# OUR LABOR OF LOVE

## A Romanian Adoption Chronicle

### by Barbara and Patrick Canale

A Pine Tree Press Publication
North Country Books
Utica, NY

OUR LABOR OF LOVE

FIRST EDITION
Copyright © 1994 by
Barbara and Patrick Canale

Cover design by Kevin Cramer
Rear cover photograph by Rich D'Agostino
Center photographics by Barbara Canale

# DEDICATION

To Romania's "lost children."

May they all someday be found.

A portion of the proceeds from the sale of this book will go directly to the children in Romania's orphanages.

# ACKNOWLEDGMENTS

We would like to express our deepest gratitude to Julie Traeger and her parents, Alice and John Traeger, for all of their encouragement. Thank you also to Dail Mizerski who inspired us to write this book. A special thank you goes to Aurther Griel and Heather Robertson who spent countless hours editing the manuscript. We are also grateful to Sheila Orlin for her guidance in publishing this book. A warm thank you is extended to Kevin and Beverly Cramer who designed the cover of this book. Their kindness and words of support carried us through many difficult moments.

# TABLE of CONTENTS

# Introduction

Of all the Christmases that I can remember, one will stay in my thoughts forever. The memories of Christmas of 1989 will be with me forever. Like many Christmases before, we woke up all alone that morning. It was snowing so peacefully outside while Pat and I sat beside the Christmas tree and exchanged presents. Our families were in different faraway places, celebrating with their other families. That Christmas the sounds of children's laughter and joyful screams of excitement were missing, sounds and scenes that our parents must have cherished. We wondered to ourselves, would we ever know and hear these sounds of children at Christmas? We are infertile and had just spent the last six years of our lives struggling to overcome the burden that God had so unfairly bestowed upon us. We had already resolved that we would never come to hear these sounds. To us, children were to be seen as well as to be heard, but this would remain a mirage, a broken dream forever.

Meanwhile, half way around the world, in the tiny Eastern European country called Romania, the people were fighting the injustices that had been a part of their daily lives for decades. While we were battling our fate with modern medical procedures, the people of Romania were battling theirs with guns and words. Little did we know then that someday our worlds would meet. In looking back to 1989, I realize that we shared something in common with the people of Romania. We both had been suffering in silence and had become emotionally scarred forever.

While our Christmas and other days were spent longing for the joyful sounds of children, thousands of Romanian institutions were warehousing children whose rooms echoed their silent screams. This is our story about how we went in search of one of these so called "lost" children of Romania in the summer of 1991.

-Barbara Canale

# Chapter 1
# The "I" Word

It was the hottest day of the year in July of 1983 when Pat and I pledged our love, honoring each other in sickness and in health, for richer or poorer, until death do us part. We declared during the wedding ceremony and to all of our family and friends that we would gladly accept children in our lives. Knowing that we wanted a family, we thought we would keep with the family tradition and start one right away. Pat and I both had college educations and good jobs. I ran a Nuclear Medicine Department in a small country hospital and Pat worked in the computer industry. Being financially stable eliminated the typical money issues that younger couples faced. We were emotionally stable. We went to church every Sunday. We considered ourselves religious people and always believed that God would provide. We paid our taxes, and were good law abiding citizens, except for Pat's occasional speeding violations. What could possibly be better for us than to move into our first home and plan for that baby?

We decided to live in Syracuse, New York, my home-town. I knew Pat for a long time; we were friends for five years before our wedding. I was twenty-five years old when we married, Pat was twenty-six. We built a modest home in a young and growing community, where our neighbors were just like us, professional people in their late twenties with similar dreams and goals. As time went on however, our dreams and goals were not flourishing the way theirs were. It was frustrating for us not to have achieved a pregnancy during the first year of our marriage, and it became inevitable that we seek medical help.

We went to one doctor who then sent us to yet another doctor, and finally ended up being referred to an infertility specialist. We chose to stay with that specialist because he made us feel as if there was hope for us to someday have a baby. We put all of our faith and trust in him. He was in his fifties and his middle-eastern accent was hard to understand. The doctor boasted about all of the baby photos that hung on his walls claiming to have gotten all of those "infertile" couples pregnant. He promised to do the same for us. I could envision our photograph on display in his office as well. He told us that it wouldn't be easy, and it would cost money, and we would have to do everything his way or no way. We didn't particularly care for his bedside manner, but if he helped us get pregnant, we could accept it.

As we left his office on that initial visit his words rang in our ears and in our hearts for days, months and even years, that "we would be pregnant by the end of the year." We always maintained that if we continued to be hopeful and strive forward, eventually that baby would come to us. That baby became the object of our desire, and was all consuming. It was as if we ate, drank, and slept on baby-making. We read every article on infertility that we could get our hands on, we listened to everyone's story on what we could try next, and what we should or shouldn't be

4

doing. Pat and I were on information overload. We didn't really care, because we would do anything, and would put ourselves through anything, just to get that baby. We became the couple with the "I" word problem. It was difficult to tell people about our infertility, and we often joked about Hester Prin who wore the scarlet letter "A" for adultery. We wore a big "I" for infertility. If Pat and I were out in public and wanted to discuss our infertility, we would rather die than to actually say that word. It was so much easier to say, "Do you want to talk about the "I" word?"

The doctor tested us for everything imaginable. We had many different types of blood tests. When those tests had normal results, we began the grueling process of infertility tests. I had a laporoscopy, hysterosalpingogram, endometrial biopsy, and post coital test to name a few. Each test brought its own realm of pain, embarrassment and disappointment. Eventually our doctor convinced us that we should try artificial inseminations, but only after one year of charting daily morning temperatures. The words artificial insemination sounded repulsive to me, and the act was demoralizing, yet if it would allow us to have a baby, it would be worth it.

Necessary provisions were arranged at work to implement our new strategy. That in itself was a major task to accomplish each and every month. It would be embarrassing to explain to our co-workers about those procedures, so we decided to tell only our managers why we would be missing so much time from work. My boss was understanding, and though she was pregnant with her second child, her condition didn't bother me, because she was so sensitive to my

5

needs. She confided to me that she also experienced difficulties in conceiving her babies. She never once underestimated what I was going through. After all, she had children, I didn't. Nevertheless, there was a common bond between us, and I felt a real closeness to her. Her encouragement, suggestions, empathy, and understanding were greatly appreciated.

In October 1984, we put our names on Catholic Charities waiting list for an adoption. We were told that we would have to wait three to four years for a healthy white infant. We knew we couldn't wait that long for a child and prayed that we could conceive one sooner. If we didn't have to wait so long and pay the high agency fees we would have taken a baby home with us the day we filed our application.

I hated the words, artificial insemination so much I wouldn't use them, but opted to use the abbreviation instead. I quickly dis-covered that it was up to me to make these unbearable circumstances as pleasant, and as comfortable as I could if I was going to be participating in them for some time. The process entailed daily temperature recordings to chart my cycle in an effort to predict when my follicles might release the egg. I was taking an oral medication called clomid, which helped my body to stimulate the follicle production.

At approximately one week prior to ovulation, I would drive into the city, which was a sixty-mile round trip, for daily ultrasounds to watch my follicles grow and develop. That would enable my doctor to determine the best possible time for the actual insemination to occur. When the time was right, Pat would meet me at the doctor's

6

office. We would sit in an office full of
pregnant women, and wait for our names to be
called. The anticipation was immense. A
nurse would call Pat in from the waiting room
and she would slowly shake a specimen cup in
front of him (and everyone else in the waiting
room) as if to tease him. The nurse would
direct him to the bathroom and announce, "It's
time to do your thing." It may sound funny to
people who have not had to experience public
masturbation in an office bathroom, but I was
humiliated for Pat, and I knew how
demoralizing it was for him.

Pat later told me about times when he
would just stand in the bathroom and look in
the mirror and think to himself, "What in the
hell am I doing?" Then he said he would
quickly realize he was just procrastinating
and he would wonder how long he was expected
to be in the bathroom. Then he would wonder
if there was a line of pregnant women standing
in line outside the door, waiting for him. He
wondered if anyone could hear him. After Pat
had his specimen, he thought he couldn't walk
out holding a cup of sperm and smile. He also
worried about what type of expression he
should have on his face. (Should it be a
pleasant one?) I can't believe that we
actually did inseminations for as long as we
did. Looking back on it, my part in that
ordeal was not nearly as traumatic as Pat's.
The procedure itself was not that bad. It was
the impact of the emotions that were
associated with it that upset me the most.

A few days after the inseminations I would
receive injections of HCG to help a pregnancy
along if there was one. The injections were
taken in vain because there never was a
pregnancy. After a while, I began to doubt
the inseminations, and the realization of

never achieving a pregnancy was becoming more and more evident. There were times when I couldn't accept that the inseminations were not working, because we had been doing everything right for so long. Pat even quit smoking, and we both stopped drinking, but nothing we did seemed to help except M&M candies. Hot fudge sundaes also helped get me through the depression, but it also allowed me to gain an extra thirty pounds. After six months of AI we did six months of AI with the cup method. That method held the sperm in the cervix area by a plastic cup which resembled a thick diaphragm. After that didn't work, we did another six months of intrauterine inseminations, and when that too failed, we did another six months of intrauterine inseminations with washed sperm. Nothing worked for us. We tried everything and nothing worked. We didn't try donor inseminations because it was something that Pat was never comfortable with.

We were emotionally exhausted, as well as financially drained. We were responsible for paying for all of that medical expertise which didn't work, since our medical insurance company wouldn't cover an infertility work-up that was considered "elective." Pat and I had to cough up $10,000 for pain and humiliation and no baby. Of course it was the holidays when the bill was due, and I resented paying it because I did my part. I couldn't help wondering when the baby would come. Our last insemination was on Christmas morning of 1987. Maybe we subconsciously planned it that way, or maybe it was the icing on the cake. I recall so vividly that morning as if it were yesterday when the nurse came to get us in the waiting room, and waved her full-length mink coat in our faces and said, "This is what

Santa left me, what did he leave you?" She
actually made fun of us when I told her that
Santa left me an electronic thermometer. If
she had taken her temperature every morning
for the past three or four years she would be
glad to get one too. I couldn't stop thinking
about that mink coat, and I wondered if I paid
for it with my $10,000. Then we were expected
to enjoy the rest of our day. Christmas day
was difficult for us to enjoy when we started
it off with humiliation, and ended it by
hearing comments like, "Christmas is for
children." I didn't realize that Jesus was
born just for children.

It was hard to accept that we had battled
our way through four years of medical
treatments and still we had no baby. We
weren't progressing on our adoption list and
we discovered that infertility had devastating
effects on us as a couple. We had built high
and mighty walls around us for protection
against the fertile society in which we lived;
interaction with fertile people was nearly
impossible. We hated to listen to them talk
about their children and childbirth. What was
it about parenthood that made every adult want
to discuss every aspect of their tykes? We
couldn't understand why they were unable to
talk about politics, religion, or the weather.
In our neighborhood, we were the only couple
who didn't have children. We couldn't
understand the world our neighbors and friends
lived in and they couldn't understand ours.

We decided to move out of that
neighborhood but were at a loss as to where to
go. Sad and lonely, our thoughts turned to
moving west to live in the solitude of
Colorado's mountains, but we were not quite
ready to leave our families who all lived in
New York State. Even though they didn't

9

understand our infertility, we felt they would always love us. At times we found ourselves angry at our families because they didn't give us support in our infertility struggle. It wasn't until much later that we learned most families of infertile children don't know how to offer support. We found ourselves limiting our visits at family get-togethers and avoided reunions all together. From time to time Pat and I looked at our nieces and nephews with envy because we wanted a clone of them.

Infertility had turned our lives upside down, but no one else could see it. We were bitter that we were robbed of parenthood. I felt angry and sad every time someone announced a pregnancy. It seemed as if all pregnant women and new mothers hung out in shopping malls, so I found it easier to avoid the malls completely and shopped from catalogs instead. Seeing pregnant couples in love reminded me that I was not yet pregnant. I was jealous of them and sad for me. I wondered if I would ever have a daughter who could be dressed in the clothes my mom had saved for her granddaughter. I never considered how our parents felt knowing that we might never be able to give them grandchildren because I was too consumed in my own grief.

We found ourselves withdrawing from our fertile friends. Instead we developed wonderful friendships with "safe" people. Frank and Johann were safe because they were much older than us with children already in college. Their friendship was not threatening to us because we were not weighed down with repetitious stories about their children. Because they were in their fifties, we never had to worry about hearing, "Guess what, we're pregnant!" We were able to have intellectual conversations and get away for weekends together. We were making frugal attempts to rectify the enormous loss of control we felt due to our infertility by choosing who our friends would be.

We never felt so powerless until we were infertile. We realized that no matter how hard we worked to achieve a pregnancy, it was something we simply had no control over. It was extremely frustrating for us and we decided to try to get back some control of our lives by making decisions. This trivial process actually allowed us to gain back some of the self-confidence we had lost over the past four years during our medical treatments.

Even though I still yearned for a baby, I also longed to have our normal lives back. I knew our lives would never again be the way they were, but it was time to pay more attention to Pat and less attention to making a baby.

# Chapter 2
# Letting Go

In January 1988 we began to realize that we needed a break from the medical procedures. Actually, we knew deep down in our hearts that it was not going to work for us, but we couldn't bring ourselves to say, "Quit." After all, we had been very committed to it and it was all we had been doing for several years - we had done too much to give up. (Quitting is for losers, and that we are not.) We both were, and still are, very goal-orientated individuals. It was not that we ever lost sight of our goal; it was the methods in which we were attempting to achieve our pregnancy that was driving us to the edge. We didn't know what else to do. In light of the fact that we had such an enormous medical bill to pay, it made a lot of sense for us to stop temporarily, to evaluate our situation, and to rationally make some decisions about our future. For the past several years of living only for inseminations, Pat and I had forgotten how to enjoy life. We became so obsessed with baby making, that we rarely would stop to appreciate all of the good things we had going for us. We felt that after all that we had been through, it was time to step away from the medical procedures. So that was what we did.

I decided to leave my job and return to school on a full time basis and obtain a B.S. degree in Health Care Administration. I honestly wanted the degree more for personal satisfaction than anything else, yet I also knew that there was a possibility that I might never be a mother. I knew I had to devote my life to something and it might as well be a career. Before classes started, Pat and I took a fabulous vacation to Jamaica. We flew first class to an all-inclusive resort for couples only, no children allowed. That was just what our doctor should have ordered. It gave us an opportunity to step away from all of the ordinary and routine things that we became caught up in at home. The journey had allowed us to start to enjoy ourselves, our marriage, and our friendship again. The only thing that was left behind was our infertility.

School was a breeze compared to working full time and concentrating on achieving a pregnancy. Attending classes gave me just the break I needed. Because infertility was so damaging to my self esteem, it was refreshing for me to have confidence in myself again. I knew I would be successful in my school work, whereas in infertility I was uncertain whether or not I would ever be successful. Once again, I had control over my life and I felt alive. Yet, deep down inside, I couldn't get the control over my emotions the way I would have liked to. There was still a void and sadness that we felt by being childless. By that time all of our neighbors were pregnant, some for the second or even third time. I found it more and more difficult to even look at a baby, and would become panic stricken every time I came across a pregnant woman. I realized the cold facts that the odds were not in our favor for me to ever be pregnant. This death, this loss seemed too great for me to endure. I was sad that I might never be able

13

to tell my husband or my parents that we were expecting a baby. It was devastating to think of never experiencing pregnancy, and wearing a maternity dress – never knowing what it was like to have a baby grow inside of me, and feel it move for the first time. I might never know childbirth. If all of that was not bad enough, we were surrounded by news reports on television about people who kill their kids, abuse their kids, and hate their kids. (Had it really taken me this long to realize that life is not fair?)

The plight of infertility exposes one's self to a number of compromising and threatening situations. Being invited to baby showers was one such drudgery. In fact, for me it was the ultimate nightmare. On one occasion I was invited to a neighbor's baby shower, and found myself crying for two days after receiving the invitation. Somehow, I forced myself to go out and buy one of those soft, cuddly outfits and wrap it lovingly with a baby rattle in the big yellow ribbon. I actually dreamed about that outfit for several nights. I never did make it to that shower. I ended up apologizing to my neighbor for having forgotten the day, when actually I sat by the window and watched each and every neighbor walk down the street, carrying beautiful packages for the expectant mother. The realization kept haunting me that I would never be an expectant mother; there would never be any baby showers for me. I felt so empty and hollow inside. With each and every invitation came my own personal struggle to buy, wrap, and deliver each gift. Every step was such a painful duty for me, and I was unsure of just how long I could continue to give.

With each passing year, Mother's Day

14

became a painful and constant reminder that I was still not a mother. One Sunday I recalled the priest in our church requesting all mothers to stand up for a special blessing. I was so resentful by it that I had to leave church so that no one would see how upset I was.

It was soon thereafter that Pat and I attended a conference in Ithaca, New York for infertile couples. I was surprised to know that there could be such a thing. It was as if someone threw us a life-saver. We were so glad that we attended for we learned that we were not alone in the struggle that those around us failed to understand. We realized that our families and friends were not the only ones who were unable to give us the support we hoped for, because they didn't know how. There were many other infertile couples who lacked family support as well. Suddenly, Pat and I no longer felt so alone, and so alienated. We started attending regular meetings at a local support group, and learned many coping strategies.

It was at one of those meetings that we met Becky and Steve. They were a lot like us, and we honestly needed to socialize more with couples like ourselves, who knew and understood the pains of infertility. It was refreshing to be with another couple who wouldn't make us uncomfortable with unbearable comments like, "When are you going to have a baby, you have been married so long, what are you waiting for? Don't you know how?" Becky and Steve occupied the emptiness that we felt in our lives, and then some. They were to become very good friends. Reflecting back, I don't think I could have grown as an individual in my infertility struggle if it were not for the support and love they gave us. It was rejuvenating to be with them. They allowed us to be ourselves, and that was something our "fertile" friends couldn't do.

Our fertile friends never realized what they were doing to us. For example, Joan, a friend of mine from college would call me on the phone, and each and every time she would always ask if I was pregnant yet. I began to dread talking to her because I knew I would have to explain why I was still not pregnant. Eventually Joan became pregnant and I found it impossible to be around her. I was not even able to attend my sister-in-law's bridal shower; I knew Joan would be there and simply found it easier to avoid her than confront her. I knew that sounded absurd to some people, but the insensitive comments she made continued to echo in my mind for years after they were spoken.

The worst story she told me was about a wedding she was in. She showed me a photograph of the wedding and indicated that one of the sisters of the bride was not a "real" sister because she was not a blood relative, she was adopted. The poor girl was not considered family because she was not of their "blood?" I knew deep down in my heart that if I ever did have a baby, it would probably be adopted, and I wanted my child to be a part of a "real" family regardless of blood. Actually, we had heard so many heartless, thoughtless, and insensitive comments, that it made us quite bitter. We were aware that we were bitter, and we hated that.

On July 19, 1989, my thirty-first birthday, my sister-in-law announced to me that she was pregnant. Just a few short months later on Pat's birthday, my brother's wife proclaimed to us that she too was

16

pregnant. That was very difficult for us to hear, especially on our birthdays, because those days symbolized that we were getting older. Our biological clocks were ticking louder than ever, and still we didn't have a baby, and just how in the world were we going to get one?

As time rolled on, we built a new home in a new neighborhood, and I finally received my degree, so actually we had accomplished quite a bit. A new year, 1990, was right around the corner and we were compiling a list off all our accomplishments, which sadly didn't include adding a baby to our household. We really felt a void and decided that if we couldn't fill it with a baby, we would fill it with other things. I bought myself a sexy little sports car; I didn't want to buy a station wagon with wood paneling along the side when I could drive a car that had the ability to reach 120 mph. I didn't have to worry about fitting a car seat in it. We went a little crazy and it was fun spending money. After all, we didn't have to worry about saving money for college educations. We could spend that money on ourselves. It may seem a little greedy, but at the time it was essential for us to know that there was a positive side to our infertility.

We also acquired the absolutely best thing in the world, a dog. Not just any dog, but a high-strung English Springer Spaniel. We named her Sparkey. She really helped me deal with infertility, believe it or not. She was like my baby - at least I treated her that way. She was exactly what I needed to allow myself the opportunity to nurture her. She also required a lot of attention and care; therefore, my idle time was spent in a constructive manner, focused on teaching and

17

loving the dog. Every morning at the crack of
dawn, Sparkey and I would go on our special
walk and enjoy the peacefulness and splendor
of the day. I thought it was strange that it
was the first time in a long time that I
enjoyed anything, and it was given to me by
the dog. I could tell Sparkey absolutely
anything and she always listened to me, and
gave me her unconditional love. When I was
sad, it was the dog who would make me glad
again. She was very therapeutic.

We also started to see an infertility
counselor, who was instrumental in helping us
deal with our feelings and emotions. It was a
very difficult decision for us to see a
counselor. We thought people who needed
professional counseling were either weak or
sick. Since we were neither, we felt inclined
to give counseling a try. Because our
counselor also struggled with infertility she
was able to understand exactly how we felt.
She assured us that the wide spectrum of
emotions associated with infertility were all
normal.

On my thirty-second birthday in July 1990,
we declared ourselves "child-free" but we
actually felt childless. The affirmation of
our status was a conscious effort to allow us
to move on in our infertility struggle. (The
word "childfree" means we have accepted that
our lives won't include children and we
welcome the decision to be that way. The word
"childless" means we still want children.) We
accepted the fact that we were not going to
have our own biological children and we gave
ourselves time to mourn that loss. Our
families were unable to comprehend it when we
told them we were mourning the loss of a child
that we would never have. We began giving
away "things" that we saved to give to our

children - things that had a special meaning to us. I gave my sister's daughter my favorite music box, and my brother's son the silver cup I wanted my child to drink from. Giving these things away symbolized to us our willingness to let go and move on. It was a very sad time for me though, because it seemed as if everyone had babies except us. We were infertile people living in a fertile society.

Our new neighborhood was beginning to grow quite rapidly. We felt as if we actually belonged there. Our neighbors were like genuine friends, almost closer than family in some ways, and many of them didn't have children. The ones that did have kids never made us feel bad for not having them. We were lucky to have these people included in our lives. That was a welcome change from the old neighborhood. Something that we positively needed was support, and we felt that and a whole lot more from living in that community.

Pat and I were discovering that because of infertility, we were developing keen problem-solving skills. Because of our struggle as a couple, we had become very close as a couple, and enhanced our communication skills. We had the ability to analyze problems and solve them with a greater degree of insight. It was nice to be able to see the silver lining in the big old gray cloud that had been looming over our heads for the past several years.

The summer of 1990 was perhaps the most difficult for us since letting go of our dreams to have our own children. We were desperately searching for what we were going to do with the rest of our lives. That could be a very long time. We were unsure of how long we could continue the shopping spree. We thought we would buy a retirement home and use it for a second vacation home. I couldn't keep myself from thinking that we were just too young to already own a retirement home. I assumed that I would retire from my management position at the American Red Cross and some day live in Florida with all of the other retired folks. We had already traveled all over the entire United States and a recent trip to England left us thirsting to see the rest of Europe so we thought we would spend more time traveling.

Still, we felt lost, like we didn't belong anywhere. We felt like outcasts in society, because we didn't have children. I couldn't stop thinking about how we spent Christmas day of 1989. Pat and I had nowhere to go, so we had taken the dog for a long walk in the woods. We were very lonely. We didn't want to be lonely for the rest of our lives. Even though Christmas of 1990 was five months away, I was already dreading not having anywhere to go or anything to do but walk in the woods again with Pat and the dog, my two best friends. We started to talk about our fears, and something strange happened to the conversation. We thought less about the "I" word and started talking more about the "A" word, adoption. We wanted to investigate that taboo topic and take the mystery out of it.

# Chapter 3
# The "A" Word

Autumn was always our favorite time of year. Even though it meant the end of summer, and the days were to grow shorter, the brisk air reminded us that we were alive. Although we didn't embrace the "A" word, we made it a part of our vocabulary. We knew we had three alternatives; agency, private, or foreign adoption. We eliminated foreign adoption because we didn't think we could afford to travel around the world to a land we knew little about. The concept of an international adoption was too new for us and unfortunately we disregarded that option. To us, there was no other alternative since we had been on Catholic Charities waiting list for six years, and our names wouldn't come up for adoption until we were in our mid forties which was another ten years. In September, 1990, we hired a lawyer to help us with a private adoption. It sounded more risky than anything we ever thought we would consider, but if that was our only option, then we had to do it if we wanted a baby.

The investigation process began by learning the ins and outs of private adoption. We frequently visited our local library and bookstores in an attempt to educated ourselves, as we were starved for information. Most importantly, it was essential for us to be certain that adoption was really what we wanted to do. We felt that experiencing

pregnancy was not the most important thing in
the world, but parenting was. For us the need
to parent was burning at the depth of our
souls. We knew that our lives wouldn't be
complete if we missed out on parenthood.
Where our child came from was no longer
important to us. The only thing that mattered
was finding a baby for us to love and nurture.
We felt we were making the decision to adopt
at the right time, yet there was still
something unsettling about a private adoption,
because so many things could go wrong. Our
greatest fear with a private adoption was
having a birth mother change her mind. I knew
that would break my heart and my spirit. I
wondered how I would react if I was required
to hand back a baby to a birth mother who
changed her mind after I had already bonded
with the child. There were so many unanswered
hypothetical questions that bothered me. Our
attorney, who also adopted her children, knew
what we were going through, because at one
time or another, she also experienced similar
feelings. Although it was comfortable working
with that lawyer, we found her fees were
astronomical - $160 per hour. I usually talk
slow and have a tendency to ramble, but
because that lawyer's fees were exceptionally
high, she taught me how to speak quickly and
to the point.

Basically, that lawyer was to teach us how
to locate an adoptable child somewhere in the
United States. We had to have a homestudy
completed, and compile a photo album of our
family to present to a potential birth mother,
along with a letter to her describing what Pat
and I were like. Lastly, we needed to run
advertisements in the newspapers around the
country in hopes that someone would call us.
All of that was emotionally exhausting and

financially draining.

We started the process by completing the homestudy, and that was not entirely the most pleasant experience I have ever had. Actually, it was quite humiliating, and I resented being put in the spotlight where I was required to prove to total strangers (the social workers) that Pat and I would be acceptable parents. We had to substantiate most of our well-thought-out answers with examples. I had to discuss how I would raise a child in the event of Pat's premature death. Such questions left me fatigued. No one could do more soul searching than infertile couples about whether or not to pursue adoption. Most of us analyze for years and years each and every step we take to achieve our families. I couldn't understand why adoptive parents must be scrutinized so strenuously. We were aware from talking to other adoptive couples that not all homestudies were conducted in the same manner that ours was.

When our social workers came to our home to perform the ritual, Pat and I were nervous wrecks. I got up at 5 a.m. to bake home-made blueberry muffins, knowing that the aroma of those goodies, with fresh-brewed coffee would give me something pleasant to look forward to. The social workers asked us questions regarding our financial situation, ethical and moral beliefs. After several hours of such questions, we then had to give a tour of our home. The process was an uneasy one that made me a little spiteful for having to do it. It was one step down, many more to go.

We spent many endless hours compiling a marketable photo album. All of the neighbors and our families helped out and before we knew it, it was complete and something to be proud of. We selected our favorite photographs of our closest family members and friends. We spent countless hours writing captions for each picture so that the album told a story about our hobbies and interests. I would often look at it and think if I was out looking for a family, I would choose us.

Our letters were difficult to write since I hated the feeling that I was selling and marketing myself. I was boasting about what a wonderful person I am, and what a wonderful mother I would be based on all of my accomplishments. I am not a boastful type of a person; I am reserved, and dislike talking about my accomplishments. Pat and I somehow managed to write wonderful letters depicting what great parents we would be.

The next step was to place ads in the newspapers. We installed a second phone line in our home and we referred to it as the "baby line." The line was actually installed for over a month, yet we were unable to place the ads in the paper. It was apparent that even though we desperately wanted a baby, we were not anxious to broadcast across the country that we couldn't conceive our own children. There was something unnatural about looking for a baby in the want ads. It just didn't feel right. However, we were prepared to do what we had to do to get a baby.

Talking to other couples who adopted privately gave us a clearer picture of the many difficulties we could possibly face. Some of their experiences were so disturbing, we were unsure of whether or not to continue pursuing a private adoption. We heard many stories about couples getting obscene phone calls on their baby lines. I knew that if our baby line rang, it was up to me to take the call. I was uncertain how devastated I would be if we received a prank call. We were also warned that often potential birth mothers would call several times and after they got our hopes up, they change their minds. The ultimate nightmare was when birth mothers wait until the last minute to decide to keep the baby and the financial loss, not to mention the emotional loss, would be ours. Our lawyer informed us that we could stand to loose at least $20,000. The realization of the many risks involved were becoming too great for us to bear. Our fears were heightened when we saw Hollywood's version of private adoption in the movie "Immediate Family."

That dilemma climaxed in late September 1990 as we landscaped our home. I remember digging holes ten times the size that they should have been because I had so much frustration and anxiety over our adoption process. I had never even held a pick before, let alone swung one to dig holes for trees. When our landscaping project was completed, we still had not made our decision whether or not to continue the adoption process. We struggled feverishly for months trying to make a decision about just how far we were willing to go to get a baby. I was so afraid of being hurt again. After all, I had put so much faith, time, and money into the infertility treatments, I was unsure of how much more heartache I could take.

We hosted the infertility support group's Christmas party of 1990, and it was at that party when I realized there were three couples in my home that evening that had tried private adoptions. All three had birth mothers change their minds after the babies were placed in the adoptive parents' home. That shattered my dreams of adopting, because I was not emotionally prepared to hand back a baby. I had convinced myself that something like that could never happen to us, and even though I knew in the back of my mind that there was a chance that it could happen, I wouldn't allow myself to believe that it would. I created that defense mechanism to allow us to continue on schedule, and I hoped that we could have a baby in our arms before my birthday in July.

Christmas reinforced how nice it would be to have children in our family, and we felt prepared to fight the world to get ourselves the family that we had been dreaming of for the past seven years. We started "pumping" each other up, to get tough, to get mean and rough or whatever it was going to take. We knew it was up to us to find our own baby.

Our goal was to write an attractive ad and run it throughout the entire state of Texas until we received a response. Our attorney recommended we search for a baby in Texas because she had many successful clients who adopted babies from that state. It took us forever to do it, but eventually we broke down and did it. The ads were to cost us over $300 per week to run. We never received any obscene phone calls, but we did get a lot of wrong numbers. Every time that the phone rang, our bodies shook with fear. I would either have a mouthful of food, or be on the other phone talking to my mom, and have to hang up quick in a panic-stricken state, just to get a wrong number. One time I was so angry that I yelled at the poor person on the other end of the phone.

Then one Friday night the phone rang with a real birth mother on the line. I talked to her for over an hour, and I really liked her a lot. I thought I would dislike her, but I found myself wanting to know all about her. I was bonding with the woman who could provide us with the child that we had been dreaming of for so many years. Pat sat beside me, holding my hand, longing to feel the connection I was experiencing through the telephone lines.

The nice women never called back. So much for our "Immediate Family."

# Chapter 4
# Chasing a Faraway Dream

As the leaves on the trees were changing into brilliant colors, our hearts were undergoing a vibrant transformation of their own. We watched a heart-warming story on television about American couples who went to Romania to adopt children that were discovered in orphanages. I soon realized that it was another option for us. We felt certain that with so many children available for adoption in Romania we would be more successful there. We didn't want to compete with the thousands of childless couples for the limited numbers of babies in America. We were not going to be scared, timid little cowards any more. I felt determined that we were going to find our baby even if I had to die trying. I knew that if I had a hard time running an ad in a newspaper, I would have a lot of trouble flying off to a third world Communist country. However, I couldn't stop thinking about it either. Whenever I thought about it, I would finish my thought with, "I know I am not that strong. Or am I?"

On February 1, 1991, our infertility support group featured speakers who adopted from foreign countries at the monthly meeting. We had never given an international adoption much thought until that meeting. There were two couples who adopted children from South America, a man who adopted from Korea, and a woman who adopted from Romania. They told their stories with so much emotion, I had chills running up and down my spine during the entire meeting. It was incomprehensible what anguish those people went through just to get a baby. A few times during the meeting, I noticed tears were rolling down not only my face, but the faces of others as well. By the time we left the meeting I was convinced we were not strong enough to do something that courageous. I cried on the car trip home because, though I knew we were too frail to get involved in such an enormous undertaking, I knew in my heart that it could be the solution to our adoption dilemma. I didn't know where we could we draw our strength from. We wondered what could be the motivating factor to enlighten and help us forge ahead with an international adoption.

We tape-recorded the meeting so that we could listen to the tapes over and over again. Each time we listened, we came a little closer to saying we might be able to do it. Then we would say, "No way, we're crazy, we can't do it, let's forget it." That weekend we browsed in a nearby shopping mall and stumbled upon a book on Romania. The store's manager informed us that they didn't stock books on Romania, and he was surprised to have the one I found. I took that as a sign from God, that we were supposed to go to Romania to find the baby that we had been longing for. Pat didn't feel that way. He said it was a coincidence. I started praying to God every minute of the day. I asked God to give me a sign to let me know that I was doing the right thing. I asked him to turn my silver rosary beads into gold rosaries. Looking back at it, I was really asking for a miracle in itself by asking for the color change. (What was I thinking?) We became obsessed with Romania, and thirsted for information about the country, and its adoption laws. We spent countless hours at the library researching Romania. In school we never did such an intensive and thorough research job, but this was different. We copied stories from microfilm, old newspapers, and old magazines. We compiled a scrap-book, and knew someday our child could look at it and know that we put a lot of time and energy into researching the adoption process in an attempt to find him or her.

It was important for us to understand the plight of the Romanian children. The story came to light when we began to understand the kind of evil man and savage dictator Nicolae Ceausescu was. He came to be Romania's Communist ruler, rising to power in the late 1960's. It was during his reign that his greed and lust for power eventually became so destructive that it crippled the entire country. In his quest to increase Romania's economic growth (by increasing the population), the Ceausescu regime mandated that women, regardless of their marital status, have as many children as possible. Women with less than five children were subjected to heavy taxation or possible imprisonment. Many families were unable to feed themselves, and were forced to institutionalize their children for their own survival in that poverty stricken country. It was not until the death of Ceausescu in December of 1989, that the world discovered the over abundance of children warehoused in Romanian orphanages. The conditions in most orphanages were appalling. Many of the children were neglected, abused, and forgotten. When thousands of Westerners and Europeans poured into Romania to adopt these orphans, the children who were lucky enough to go to good homes were referred to as the "found children." The others left behind were considered the "lost children." Many of the lost children needed to be found, and it was up to us to go to Romania and find our child.

We joined an organization for couples interested in Romanian adoptions. The paperwork received from that special group helped us to start working on the formal paperwork necessary to finalize a foreign adoption. Our excitement was building, yet there was something inside us questioning our ability to accomplish such an enormous undertaking. However, at that time, a Romanian adoption felt better to us than a private adoption in America. In a way, it sounded crazy that anyone could be more comfortable with going to Romania with all its uncertainties. We felt drawn to the Romanian children for some unknown reason, and I would shudder when I thought about the thousands of orphaned children desperate for a good home. I knew I had just the home for a Romanian child. We felt good about adopting from a country where we would actually make a difference in the outcome of the child's life. Everyone I talked to seemed to be interested in the Romanian orphans, but I was willing to go and get one of them.

In the early part of spring, we heard about a young expectant mother who was thinking about making an adoption plan locally. Once again, I was excited about a private adoption, because it sounded so promising. It was like a dream come true. We were making plans to travel halfway around the world and comb Romania's orphanages looking for a baby, when there was one practically on our door step. We began making plans for a nursery as well as the many necessary arrangements required for a new baby. We had so many decisions to make! We had to decide what type of bottles and formula to use. We made lists of things to buy for the baby. We even thought about names for the child.

I informed my boss at the American Red Cross about my plans to pursue the baby. I was allowed to cut back my hours to only twenty per week. It gave me the time I needed to get ready for a new baby as there was so much work that needed to be done. There was a possibility that the local adoption could fall through, yet I was trying to put that out of my mind, always thinking positive. I began to imagine what it would be like having a baby in the house, daydreaming and fantasizing about what the baby would look like, and who it would grow up to be.

My sister offered to give me all of her hand-me down baby clothes and furniture. That was going to help us out financially as our adoption pursuit was so costly. We were grateful for any help given to us. In addition, we were excited to get all of her baby paraphernalia because it would be fun to look at and play with while we were waiting for the baby to come. The day that Pat and I planned to drive to my sister's house to collect all of the baby essentials we received a phone call from her telling us not to come because she just found out that she was pregnant for her fifth child. She was elated, but needless to say I was not at all happy. Maybe it was the way she informed me about her condition, exclaiming that it was a miracle. She had so much joy and happiness in her voice. It was not that I was angry that she got pregnant and needed her baby things. It all boiled down to her insensitivity in selecting her words and tone of voice when she told me, or any infertile person, who had been trying desperately for years and years to have a baby. I didn't consider my sister's ability to have a fifth child a miracle. If I got pregnant after trying for close to eight years, that would be a miracle. I was so hurt by how my sister told me that I started crying on the phone. She was waiting to hear congratulations, and not hearing it made her angry. She was hurt that I was crying instead of being happy for her. She couldn't stop and think of my feelings. Pat and I went for long walks to talk about how insensitive my sister was but nothing seemed to help - not even candy.

Within 24 hours of my sister's phone call telling me about her pregnancy, we learned that the local private adoption that we were working on had fallen through. The birth mother apparently had given birth to a baby girl and decided to keep her. That was just our bad luck. We were devastated, but we quickly recovered by remembering how comfortable we still felt with Romania. My sister's "news" gave us even more determination to forge on and adopt a baby from that country. Year after year we swam in a sea of disappointments, knowing that at any moment we could easily drown. Instead of tiring from always fighting against the currents, a surge of energy engulfed us and allowed us to fight even harder than we ever thought we were capable of.

We went shopping and bought baby clothes for our new Romanian baby. We felt for the first time that we were expecting a baby. When I told my mom about my feelings of "expecting" she told me I was setting myself up to be hurt. My parents were shocked to see that a nursery was designed, and there was a crib just waiting for a baby. I could see a baby in it, but no one else could. Some of my family thought I was going off the deep end but I knew I was okay. We felt the strength we needed to go to Romania, and I knew that we would have a baby for my next birthday in July. I was sure of it.

I started attending daily mass at the Cathedral where Pat and I were married. I would ask God every day if we were doing the right thing. In my heart I sort of felt like we were doing the right thing, but I was still looking at my rosary beads every day to see if God would give me some kind of sign. I was still afraid to go to Romania. At least 1,000 other Americans had adopted there, but still I felt frail, and was unsure of how much I could endure. We thought that desperation would be enough to get us through the journey ahead. For some unknown reason, I was always looking for more. I needed that "sign from God." Then one dark and dreary day when I was praying in church, golden rays of sunlight beamed through the beautiful stained glass windows and shown all around me and my heart was full of peace. I knew that God no longer had to give me a sign to see, that I had one that I could feel. It was a sign so peaceful, that I knew I wouldn't have to second-guess again. My faith was placed in God that it would work for us in Romania. Somehow, someway, I knew there was a baby there for us, and we just had to go get it. I really felt a calling to go to Romania, because God wanted one less child to suffer in an orphanage there. We began to realize that we were uncomfortable with private adoption for a reason. God wanted us to let other couples in America adopt the babies here. We had what it

34

would take to travel to Romania to save the life of a child there. Having traveled extensively throughout the world, we hoped that we would be fine. Even though I was feeling somewhat comfortable with going to Romania, I was nevertheless, still scared. (After all, who wouldn't be just a little scared?)

On March 11, 1991, we contacted a law firm from another state who helped couples adopt in Romania. We trusted in their dependability and hired them immediately. We paid them $5,000 for their services. It included having someone meet us at the airport upon arrival in the capital city of Bucharest, locating a child with us, doing all the necessary paperwork for the courts, and seeing us off when the process was completed. It was going to be an extremely difficult process, but we were counting on the stability and knowledge of honest United States attorneys. Through our faith in God and trust in our lawyers we found that strength we were looking for in the earlier months.

We started organizing our paperwork, which turned out to be quite an ordeal. We had to gather four original copies of our birth certificates, marriage license, homestudy, social worker's license, physician's letters, police reports and criminal records, bank reference letters, personal reference letters, employment letters, our New York State pre-adoption certification, copies of the first five pages of our passports, a copy of 1040 tax form, and photographs of our home, family, and friends. We also had to have our fingerprints checked through the FBI. Most of those documents also had to be notarized and certified. We made several trips to county clerks' offices to get the documents redone

35

because they were not done correctly initially. All of our documents cost in excess of $500. We also had to pay an additional $350 to have our documents translated into the Romanian language. We got our passports, visas, and made our airline and hotel reservations.

There were several airlines which we could have flown with, but after great consideration, we chose Swissair. Because Switzerland is a neutral country their planes are less likely to be the target of international terrorism. Our airline tickets cost $3,000 and though it was expensive, it was a small price to pay for our comfort, safety, and peace of mind. When it came to selecting our hotel in Bucharest, the choice was not an easy one. The InterContinental Hotel came highly recommended by other couples who stayed there, partly because of its proximity to the United States Embassy. One drawback of staying at that hotel was the price of the room. At $126 per night, it became quite an expensive place to retreat to at the end of each day.

Things were progressing smoothly and we were very excited. We found waiting for U.S. Immigration's approval was the hardest thing to do. I wanted to leave without it. I continually reminded myself that good things come to those who wait.

There was a terrible show on television about the Romanian adoptions, insinuating that many of the babies adopted were sold to couples on the black market. That was not what we wanted to hear. We wanted to adopt a baby honestly. We didn't want to go over there to buy a child. The lawyer we hired reassured us that his staff in Romania were honest people and they wouldn't get us

36

involved with baby selling. Our lawyer used a helpful analogy that made it easier for us to understand. He said it was like being aware that drugs were sold on the streets where he lived. He had never seen it, yet he knew it was happening. If you are approached to buy drugs, you just say no. The same thing applied to Romania. Even though the television show scared us, our attorney reassured us that we could get through it.

We contacted our private adoption lawyer to inform her that we no longer needed her services as we were planning to adopt in Romania. We paid her fees which were close to $3,000. In an attempt to persuade us against going to Romania, that attorney sent us a letter from a local woman, Julie, who was volunteering her services working in Romanian orphanages with the children who were considered to be worthless to society. I read and reread that letter more than one hundred times, trying to get a feel for what Romania would be like. Julie's letter reinforced to us how essential it was for us to adopt from Romania as the children there didn't stand much of a chance of surviving. It was no particular word that she used in her letter which gave me the feeling of urgency to hurry up and get over there. Maybe it was the overabundance of children living in such poor conditions. We felt frustrated that we couldn't hop on a plane right then and get as many children as we could carry back. I called Julie's father and explained to him that I was able to read a copy of his daughter's letter and it touched a place in my heart that I never knew existed. I expressed my desire to continue reading Julie's letters as they came, so he offered to keep me informed by sending me copies of her letters.

I studied her letters as they arrived, trying to imagine what the orphanages where really like. We started to keep a scrap book of Julie's letters. I am not sure why, but if it was about Romania, we would keep it.

I spoke frequently with Julie's dad and he was so helpful in preparing me for what Romania was going to be like. He described what the countryside looked like and how the government was run. He spent countless hours coaching and encouraging me for the expedition and I will always be grateful for all of his help. In a way, I felt like I knew Julie, when in fact, I had never met her and I had no idea what she even looked like. Yet I thought about her all the time. I talked about her so much that we made plans to meet her in Romania. I was really moved by Julie's kindness and devotion to the Romanian children. We decided if we were lucky enough to adopt a girl, we would name her Juliana, the Romanian version of Julie.

On April 23, U.S. Immigration approved us for a foreign adoption by issuing us our I-171, the document which would enable us to adopt a child internationally. We were elated because it was what we had been waiting for. Immediately I contacted our lawyer who was assisting us in the process and he informed us that his staff wouldn't be able to accommodate us until May 17th. My God, I was not sure I could wait that long. I had been waiting eight years for a baby, and we were so close, the anticipation was consuming all of our patience.

At least we had time to pack and get ready. We had three huge suitcases sprawled out across the living room floor and every time we thought of something we would need, we would throw it in a bag. We chose to pack old clothes so we wouldn't be depicted as rich Americans. We were careful in the selection of our T-shirts to ensure that they were not bright colors or that they didn't have any logos on them. Our outfits were drab, and not considered to be at all fashionable, but we were not going to Romania as tourists or to impress people with how we dressed.

We started organizing a "care package" for Julie with items her dad knew she would like. We went a little overboard buying "gifts" for the Romanian people. We were advised to bring gifts to exchange for services. Gifts were needed to obtain even the most basic goods. We packed a variety of chocolates, perfumed soaps, cosmetics, jewelry, lace underwear, and stockings. All of these common staples of American life had been withheld from the people of Romania by the Communist regime. The most valued gift that we brought with us was Kent cigarettes. We also started packing baby clothes of all sizes. Because we were uncertain as to the size of the baby we would be adopting, we had to pack to accommodate all ages and sizes. Our suitcases were also filled with disposable diapers and powdered formula. We felt as if we were ready.

Our church was in the process of photographing each parishioner's family and compiling the photographs into a big family church album. Though we didn't want to have our photograph taken, we put on a happy face and smiled for the camera. I wanted them to wait for us to have our baby, but of course, they couldn't wait. I told a parishioner who was organizing the photo session about my reluctance to have our picture taken, but she encouraged us to have it taken anyway. As we were leaving she told me she was glad we were going to Romania because God had a special baby for us there, we just had to go find it. Later we discovered that our photograph didn't come out and it had to be repeated when we returned from Romania. We looked upon that incident as an angel from heaven telling us that our family was not yet complete.

I discovered a woman who lived nearby would also be adopting a baby in Romania the same time as we would. Maria and I made plans to contact each other while in Romania. It was reassuring for me to have a friend from home there, experiencing similar feelings and fears. We would have each other for support and companionship while in Romania.

On May 5th we met the attorney who was instrumental in assisting us with the adoption process. For several hours we discussed what Romania was like and how difficult the adoption process would be. He tried to prepare us for what we would encounter there, but all he did was make us wonder if Romania was really even on our planet. He made it sound as if it were a different kind of world. We were warned about the corruption that exists there, the lack of food, overabundance of disease with no medical care, and possibilities of war. By the end of our meeting, our lawyer had scared us to death, and we began to second-guess ourselves. We wondered if the trip was going to be worth risking our lives, our good marriage, and everything we ever worked for. (How good would it be to have a baby if one of us didn't make it out alive?) We actually thought about it, and made provisions in our wills in the event that we didn't survive the ordeal. We knew there was a possibility that a civil war could erupt while in Romania. We made plans to prepare alternative routes of escape in the event of war. By the time we were finished preparing for the trip, we felt certain that we had covered all angles, discussed all topics, reviewed all emergency backup plans, and left no stone unturned. That was what we thought.

May 10th was my last day of work. It was very emotional walking away from that job, because I loved it, and I was uncertain if I would be back. I was hoping I would be back, but you never know. The American Red Cross allowed me to take an unpaid leave of absence because they didn't have a maternity policy for adopting parents. In any event, it was hard to leave work that day. I continually reminded myself that it was what I had been working so hard to do. Romania was all a big unknown to me and we had no idea what we were about to get ourselves into.

I drove to my parent's house instead of going home after work that day. Maybe I needed the warm hugs that they always give, to take my sadness and apprehensions away. We sat around the kitchen table sipping hot English tea, talking about old times. It was as if that was the only thing that we could talk about without having "Romania" always pop into the conversation. It was essential to talk about funny things, happy things, anything except Romania.

When our visit was almost over, my dad became very serious as he put money in my hand with a beautiful baby card. The card read, "Something to help you buy your baby." I know the greeting card people meant to say, "Something to help you buy **for** your baby" but it was more appropriate for me without the **for**, as Mom and Dad gave me several thousand dollars. I never imagined my parents would have to help me pay for my baby, and really they didn't have to do it. My folks insisted that we take the extra cash in the event of an emergency, as it was next to impossible to wire money into Romania. I didn't want to take my parents' money. I never thought about running out of cash. Reluctantly, and thankfully, I took the money. Dad held me close to him and said, "If you are in a bind and need extra cash, you have it, so spend it, and don't think twice about it." With tears in my eyes, and a pain in my heart, I put the money in a money belt and headed for home. The thirty-mile trip home was the longest one for me as so many things raced through my mind. It was difficult to concentrate on driving when I was completely absorbed with traveling to Romania, and getting back, and returning the money to Mom and Dad. It would be terrific to tell them, "Thanks for letting me carry your money all over the world (practically) but we didn't need it so I am returning it."

Once I was home, hiding the money was foremost on my mind. However, I couldn't find a place safe enough for that much cash. Pat ended up stashing the money inside of his ski boots. I wondered what it would be like carrying $7,000 all over Hell's half acre while in Romania. To me, it was incomprehensible that only cash was acceptable there. American Express travelers checks were not even accepted. I wondered if we would be safe carrying all of that money around with us. I wondered what we would do if we got robbed. After all, we had spent $16,000 so far on adoptions and we still didn't have a baby. We would be devastated if someone stole our money and we were out $23,000. We couldn't let anything happen to those money belts! We planned to wear one around our waist with the bulk of the cash, and one

around our neck, with passports, plane tickets
and American Express travelers checks. Even
though we heard that they were impossible to
cash, we decided to bring $1,000 in checks in
the event of an emergency. We were so
paranoid about the money situation, and then
we thought about drug dealers who carry around
money like that all of the time. For us, it
was our entire life savings. If Romania
didn't work for us, or if we got robbed, we
would be financially wiped out. Regardless
whether we brought back a baby or not, we
would be broke. This adoption process was the
most costly endeavor of our lives.

We began counting down the days in
anticipation of our departure. We attended
our last church service, which was emotional
for me. I believed in my heart that the next
time that I walked into that church, I would
carry in our baby. We said our good-byes to
our friends, Becky and Steve, and again I felt
strange knowing the next time I saw them, I
would have a baby. I wondered how they would
feel about it. I hoped our fantastic
friendship would still be fantastic, and I
would try real hard not to let the baby come
between us. I knew things would be different
with a baby, I just didn't know in what ways
yet.

We spent the days prior to our departure
with Pat's parents as they offered to take
care of Sparkey for us while we were in
Romania. It was a stressful visit knowing that
the time would soon come to have to say
good-bye, and I knew it was going to kill me.
I was unsure of my feelings about my in-laws
before that day, but by the time I held each
one with tears rolling uncontrollably down my
face, my love for them grew by leaps and
bounds. I was not sure if I would ever see

43

them again, and suddenly I was real scared. For the first time I actually didn't want to leave them. Or maybe I just didn't want to go to Romania. After all, it was a very scary thing that we were about to do. I was also leaving my beloved dog. I would never forget the look on their faces as we drove off. My dog was in disbelief that we would actually leave without her. We cried nonstop all the way home.

It was not until we returned from Romania that Pat's parents told us how Sparkey searched their house for hours looking for us. It must have been such a pathetic thing to see. However, in no time at all, the love that we had given Sparkey was affectionately replaced by that of Pat's family. It turned out that they became attached to each other, and Sparkey found it equally saddening to leave them to come back home to Syracuse.

The house seemed so quiet and empty when we first walked in after leaving Sparkey. We tried not to look over at her empty food dish for we knew it would bring a tear to our eyes. We went to bed without Sparkey for the first time that night. I was sad, for I missed not having her sleeping on my feet to keep them warm. I wondered who would keep my feet warm in Romania? I was beginning to realize that I was scared out of my mind, and I had no idea about what we were getting ourselves into. Realizing that it was going to be more difficult than I originally thought, I contemplated calling it all off and cutting our losses. I went to bed bewildered but I woke up refreshed. I realized the next time I slept in this bed of mine, I would have a baby in that crib. Well, this was the day that I had to go find that baby for the crib. Most people have their baby and then must go out

and find a crib, but not us. We always seem
to do things just a little different.

# Chapter 5
# In the Nick of Time

The emotions of the prior days had drained us of much of our energy so that we actually did have a peaceful night's sleep. Our tranquil night's rest turned out to be the calm before the storm. Soon after we awoke, we were overcome with all that we had to do before our departure. I don't think that I was as excited the day I married Pat. I had more butterflies in my stomach than medicine to make it go away. We spent the better part of the day in and out of doctors' offices getting inoculations to protect us against hepatitis and various other diseases. We also needed to get a variety of syringes and needles to bring with us to test the babies blood for AIDS and hepatitis. We were warned that there were few clean hypodermic needles in Romania, and the last thing that we wanted to do was to infect a healthy infant with HIV contamination from unsterile conditions.

The morning flew by and before we knew it, the time had come to close our bags that were stuffed beyond their limits. We had read, and were told by many people that Romania was one of the poorest countries in Europe. Food shortages, especially outside of the cities, were not uncommon. Knowing that we would be traveling in the country, we packed enough food for two weeks. Our "survival kit" included peanut butter, tuna fish, cans of Spaghettios, Poptarts, soups, sausages,

46

crackers, Tang, and instant coffee. We also packed large quantities of vitamins, Tylenol, and a bottle of scotch. We had found a camping store where we purchased several varieties of prepackaged freeze-dried dinners. Pat and I had never camped a day in our lives, so we hoped they would be edible.

We split the $7,000 cash between us and loaded it into the money belts that we bought for this occasion. I wore the cash around my waist, and carried my passport, plane ticket, and a holy medal of St. Jude in a money belt hidden down my blouse. I felt so fat, and was petrified carrying so much money on me. I was a little paranoid, feeling as if the whole world knew how much cash I was hiding on my body.

It was uplifting saying farewell to our neighbors, as they had been coaching us and rooting for us all along. Their hugs were genuine and we knew we were going to miss them. As our car slowly backed down the driveway, we hesitated to drive off. We looked up at our empty house, and could almost envision our children playing on the front lawn with the neighbors' kids. Tears welled up in our eyes as the image of our waving neighbors faded in the distance. As we sped to the airport, we prayed that God wouldn't let us down now, when we needed him the most. I was very anxious to get to the airport as I pictured us missing the flight out, and I was seriously doubting whether or not I could go home and go through all of those emotions again. We didn't have to worry about missing the flight, as we arrived with plenty of time to spare. Seeing my mom and dad at the airport was a great comfort to us both. Saying good-bye to them was not nearly as sad as I thought it might be. Maybe it was because I have said good-bye to them so many times before for such extended lengths of time, I just knew I would see them again.

As our plane vanished into thin air, so did our courage. We were leaving behind the life styles we were so familiar with, and plunging into a big unknown. I ran into the bathroom and with an empty stare I looked into the mirror and asked, "Who are you, and do you know what in the hell you are doing?" Because I didn't know the answers to those questions, I can not begin to explain the trauma of the anxiety attacks I experienced on the flight to Bucharest. Initially, the trauma was over departing from Syracuse, our home. Then the trauma was when we flew out of the United States. Each time we were getting a little bit closer to building the family that we had been dreaming of for so many years.

Within 24 hours our mental visions of Romania were unfolding before our eyes as we arrived in Bucharest. Little did we know that our nightmare was just beginning. There was no welcome sign for us, but the runway full of pot holes said it all. It was a wonder that the plane was even able to land. In the distance we saw an old gray bus heading towards the plane. We both wondered if it was going to be our transportation to the terminal. When it stopped beside the plane we had our answer and waited in line for our short ride. The bus seats had been ripped out and could only accommodate fifteen standing people at a time. Upon a closer look we discovered that the bus was actually white. The worn gray color had been a result of soot that was the by-product of the engine's unfiltered fumes. We looked around to see if we could spot other adopting couples. We were surrounded by foreign tongues but did notice one British couple who had come equipped with a baby basket filled with baby supplies but no baby. To us that was a sure sign of an adopting couple. All of the passengers held onto anything they could as the bus made its way towards the terminal, shaking and rattling along the way. While I rode in the dilapidated bus, I thought about old movies I saw on television depicting Russia in wartime. I wondered if I was riding into a war zone, because the windows in the bus were either shot out or blown out. We saw dozens of young military men carrying huge rifles, all of which were undoubtedly loaded.

Tired from the flight, I closed my eyes and fell asleep. It must have been for just a brief moment, but it was long enough for me to dream that I had just stepped into the twilight zone, and traveled back in time by at least one hundred years. Once inside of the terminal building, there stood all of the passengers in a silent line waiting to be body searched. In all of the international traveling that we had done, we had never seen anything like that. Standing close to Pat, I could hear the pounding of his heart. I tenderly kissed his cheek and whispered, "A kiss for good luck." With his body close to mine, he glanced at me with eyes that told me he felt the same. No one dared to utter a word as we walked in single file through an archaic metal detector. Then we stood in another long and silent line waiting for a government official to review our passports. He was a squirrelly looking man and he reminded me of a character I once saw on "Hogan's Heroes." He was confined to a booth and I felt like I was an under-aged teen-ager trying to buy movie tickets for an X-rated film, knowing he may not sell them to me. It had become frightfully apparent to us that many intimidation practices were a way of life in Romania. Everywhere we looked we saw soldiers and government officials checking papers throughout the airport. The fear that we felt at the airport was to linger over us for the entire duration of our stay in Romania. Pat really made me laugh when he made the comment, "We are not in Kansas anymore, Toto."

When we saw our luggage we both sighed with relief. If our luggage could make the trip, then we were going to be fine. Having our "stuff" was very comforting. It meant we could eat and do a lot of things that others, who were not so lucky to have their bags, couldn't do. We were grateful to have survived the long flight into Romania and to have our bags.

We were told there would be someone from the law office waiting for us. Upon exiting the terminal we saw hordes of people hustling about. Most were taxi drivers competing with each other for customers by exchanging shouting matches and offers to carry bags. All of their olive-skinned faces seemed to blend together. Only one man stood out in the crowd, and he was Mario. His youthful and honest face had eyes so blue that I almost didn't believe that he was Romanian, until in broken English, he asked if we were the Canales. In his slender hands he held a piece of crumbled paper with our names scratched on it. He looked like a westerner, wearing acid washed jeans and a T-shirt. It was not until later that we realized it was his only outfit. He hurried us to his taxi and told us, "Adoptions no more by Friday." I thought, what does he know, and I ignored him. Within five minutes he told us he knew of two

50

fifteen-month-old infant boys whose birth mothers wanted $1,000 each. So much for avoiding the baby selling when our lawyer's people were offering us deals when we were not even out of the air terminals parking lot. We told Mario that we were really interested in locating a younger baby. He told us that we didn't have enough time to find a younger baby when the adoptions were ending on Friday. Mario told us that we should consider going back home and wait for things to cool down. After all of the planning that we had done, all of the sleepless nights, not to mention the cost both financially and emotionally that we had invested thus far, I was not prepared to have some joker tell us to turn back and fly the hell out of Romania without trying to adopt. (How could anyone just throw in the towel and quit? Certainly not me!) I was so angry to be hearing such discouraging news after only being in the country less than thirty minutes. I thought if that was any indication on how our stay in Bucharest was going to progress, then we were in for a big sorry surprise, one I didn't care to know about.

Even though I was exhausted from the flight in and sick to my stomach from Mario's terrible news, I did somehow enjoy the thirty minute ride into the city. I was trying to see everything, absorb it all, study it, so that someday I could tell my child about the country he (or she) was from. As we drove away from the airport, toward the city of Bucharest, our eyes couldn't help but notice how many patches of beautiful flowers grew abundantly along not only the roadside, but everywhere. Even the scores of run-down block-style apartment buildings we passed were outlined and dotted with beautiful flowers and trees. We had never seen such extreme beauty and ugliness coexist.

We passed a sign on the side of the road that instantly reminded us of home and is recognized throughout the free world. It was the familiar blue logo of IBM proudly advertising its presence in Romania. We then drove under a bridge that had the XEROX logo painted on it. For a moment we felt as if we were home driving into a high-tech park. As we got closer to Bucharest, we discovered that these symbols of capitalistic America, these so called household names, gave us a false sense of security. Those signs didn't appear to belong in the setting that we were in. We began to fear that like the signs, we too were out of place.

Mario dropped us off at the InterContinental Hotel and said he would call us later. The hotel was huge and the lobby was filled with couples adopting children. Some had their children already and I found it was embarrassing to look at them. They all looked so haggard and tired. I wondered how long it would take for me to look that bad.

Our room was okay, but not at all worth the $126 per night that we were paying for it. It was a typical size room, with two twin beds, both which came with a three inch sunken mattress. The chairs and dresser were from the 1950's, but it seemed to go with the over all look of "dirty and outdated." There was a nice bathroom, with a decent shower and plenty of hot water. We had our choice between heat or air-conditioning, a luxury only the rich in Romania knew. We were also pleased to have plenty of lights, and a balcony.

The door to the balcony had several bullet holes in it, scars from the revolution of 1989. We tried to picture in our minds what it was like during the revolution. We wondered how many people died in the streets that we stared at. What was life like before the revolution? It was not until we returned to America that Pat and I were to read about how much suffering those people have endured. President Ceausescu, with his Stalinist ideology, repressed individual rights, forced Romanization of ethnic minorities, destroyed the nation's architectural heritage by leveling entire sections of cities and crippled the economy with failed policies. Under Ceausescu, the poor remained poor while many wealthy intellectuals were forced into exile. Romanians couldn't travel outside their country and few westerners were allowed in. Homes lacked heat in the winter because of energy shortages, street lights were never on, and television was only broadcast for two hours a night for those lucky enough to have a television. Food markets remained bare, typewriters had to be registered with the police and soldiers were a part of every street corner.

It had been estimated that one out of every three Romanians worked for the police. People had no friends outside of their family for fear of being spied on. People constantly lived in a paranoid state of mind. Romania had been the last Eastern European Communist regime to fall. The revolution had begun when demonstrations broke out near the Romanian-Hungarian border over the lack of freedom. Ceausescu responded by calling the people for a mass rally in Bucharest to denounce the pro-democracy demonstrations. He also ordered his secret police to use deadly force to break up the peaceful demonstration in Timisoara. The result was countless people killed and wounded when his orders were carried through.

It was at the Bucharest rally that people began shouting anti-Ceasescu slogans. It had become clear to him that he no longer had the support of the people and that they would no longer remain silent. Ceausescu and his wife Elena fled the angry crowd by helicopter. Their escape was bungled when the helicopter was forced to land and rebel soldiers arrested them. The Ceausescu's were tried and found guilty of crimes against the people of Romania and were executed by a firing squad on Christmas day. Meanwhile, fighting continued in the streets throughout Romania between various military groups who sided with the people and Securitate secret police who remained loyal to Ceausescu. The battles finally subsided as the news of Ceausescu's death spread throughout the entire country.

How little did I know that the plain and colorless view from that hotel balcony would be forever etched in my mind. I never realized how often I would stare at it. I frequently wondered about the quality of lives of the people I was staring at from that window. Were they happy? How often did they go hungry? I thought about their health, and what they did if they got sick. With all of the time we had on our hands, we found ourselves examining even the oddest and most trivial aspects of everyday life in Romania. I noticed that they had little waste. We rarely saw garbage trucks. They recycled everything and would even wash out old plastic bags and hang them up to dry to reuse them. I noticed incineration occurring on the roof tops and I wondered if it was toxic. It certainly smelled awful and looked disgusting. I couldn't help wondering if they knew how dreadful it was for them to burn garbage like that. It was evident that there was little regard for the environment. The cars had no type of exhaust filter system, so inhaling the fumes could prove to be lethal. Pollution was everywhere, and seemed to be a way of life in Bucharest. For me, I hated filth, and I tried to believe that I was only going to be there on a very brief mission. I could eat that filth if it would help me get a baby so I could go home.

When the scenes from our balcony became too overwhelming, we made use of the hotel's two best assets; a television with several channels (one being CNN), and a telephone with an overseas operator. The first thing we did after we quickly clicked around the channels was to call home to Mom and Dad, all American as apple pie. Our transatlantic call was brief but uplifting and costly. Each five minute phone call that we placed to the states cost us approximately $50. I gave my parents our code: "This country is like Sparkey" and that meant it didn't appear to be that bad. If I told them that Romania was like Charlie, my family's dog when I was growing up who since passed away, that meant things were not going well and we were in trouble and in need of help. We decided to have those codes in the event that another civil war erupted and we needed to exit the country quickly without fear of taped telephone lines. We felt certain that our parents would sleep easier knowing that we were okay.

A bottle of red wine and cheese and crackers that we brought with us was our dinner. We made a little party to celebrate that we survived the trip into Romania and though we had a lot of work ahead of us, the rewards would be many. Yet there was something gnawing at us. The uneasy feeling came from Mario's warning about the doors

55

closing to the adoptions. We knew that one of the American lawyers from our firm was in Bucharest. We placed a call to him to find out what the truth was about the changing adoption laws. Unfortunately, he didn't have any good news for us. He told us that his firm tried to prevent us from going over, and his advice to us, as an American attorney, was to return home. That was absurd to me. I informed him that I had invested too much in the trip to give up and turn back. I told him that if the doors were open for one week, then I wanted his firm to help us during the time that was left, or as long as we were still there.

When the conversation was over, the tears started flowing. I thought if anyone had bad luck, it was us. Every time we plan a trip, no matter how simple or extravagant, we always encounter major or multiple dilemmas. We spent one year planning our trip to Yellowstone National Park the summer of 1988. That was the year that Yellowstone burned down and the first time in the history of the park that the Old Faithful Inn was evacuated. We were among the few people remaining in the park that were evacuated because of the threatening fire.

For over a year, people from all over the world had been flocking to Romania to adopt. In fact, one third of the world's adopted children were coming from Romania. Why did the doors have to close just as we were about to begin the adoption process? I hashed over and over in my mind all that we had gone through to get to the point we were at. I couldn't envision myself getting back on the plane and flying home without a child. I was angry at God. How could He let this happen to us? I decided that I would never go to church again; I would hate God. I was letting my

emotions take control of my better judgment.
I remembered that I had a friend praying for
us in Yugoslavia, at the shrine in Medjugorje.
I knew that God was going to take care of us.
Pat and I put our heads together and started
making plans of our own on what we were going
to do. It was after midnight and still we
couldn't sleep. We pushed our beds together,
got down on our knees, and started to pray.
At 4 a.m. we finally fell asleep. When we
awoke, my eyes were swollen from crying so
hard. The lack of sleep and the stress we
were under gave us horrendous headaches.

Saturday May 18th: At 7 a.m. we were at
the hotel's informal restaurant for a
continental breakfast, which was included in
the price of the room. The coffee was as
thick as mud and tasted terrible, but somehow
it managed to wash the dry rolls down. I
drank a lot of coffee at home; however, I
could tell that I wouldn't be drinking much
there. We switched to tea, which was imported
from China.

The restaurant was a semicircle of plate
glass windows, many of which were cracked,
with thirty foot ceilings. The one and only
wall had big old copper pots randomly hanging
for decoration. There was something that
resembled a sandwich bar in front of it where
shady men would hang out all day long. Their
business suits were outdated by American
standards but perhaps considered modern by
Eastern European fashion. They reminded us of
Chicago gangsters from the Al Capone era or
perhaps Mafia men from today's New York
underworld. If you made eye contact with any
of them, or scratched your head, they would
scurry to your table and say, "Change?" They
were fast talkers and acted slick but many of
the Americans saw right through them. We

heard the going black market exchange rate was anywhere between 150-200 lei, and those cronies were offering about 100 lei to the dollar? That was quite a ripoff.

Within the hour Mario met us in the hotel lobby and introduced us to Lili who was to be our translator. Lili was very pretty. Her long stylish raincoat masked her young and petite body. She told us that the adoption laws were changing and she couldn't help us. She had heard on the television news that anyone aiding in an adoption could go to jail. She told us to think about going home. After talking to Lili and Mario, I knew they were not going to risk their lives for us, but I felt someone had better help us.

We placed a call to the States to talk to the lawyer we had been working with for several months prior to going to Romania. Because of the time difference, we were forced to leave a message on an answering machine. Our plan was to sit in the room and wait for him to return our call. We agonized for hours while we waited for him to call us back, and passed the time by reading the room's only magazine, the International issue of Newsweek. We read every word from cover to cover including all of the advertisements. Then we watched a thirty-minute taped broadcast of CNN over and over. When we saw weather reports on CNN forecasting sand storms in central Africa, we sensed just how far from home we were. We felt so alienated that we quickly changed the channel. Instead we watched a Romanian news broadcast which gave us insight to the way news reporters cover stories in that country. The "on the scene" television cameras captured, as we watched helplessly, a house burn to the ground. The broadcast did show a man attempting to extinguish the flames with a garden hose, but his attempts were fruitless.

We became so bored, and had cabin fever so bad, we wondered how prisoners do it day in and day out. We talked about what it would be like to be in jail because we felt that was our predicament. We felt confined, and claustrophobic. We knew if we were "locked up" in America we would always have food, and we were not too sure about the food situation there. We knew in an American jail we would at least have good health care. While the health care in Romania can't be compared to western standards, we were uncertain about Romanian health practices. We were the ones who had given ourselves the "jail sentence," and we paid a lot of money for it! That was the worst part of all. We realized that we were driving ourselves crazy by all of the deep conversations that we were having, so we stopped talking and went for a walk, like a furlough.

It was so cold and rainy outside, but we wondered, how bad could it be? We could barely walk around the building without being harassed by Gypsy beggars. Every person we passed on the streets would stop and stare at us. We felt so uncomfortable that the walk was not worth it. We were soaking wet and freezing after only five minutes, so we returned to our rooms to complete our jail sentence. After we dried off we thought about sitting in the hotel lobby. We thought that maybe the change of scenery would do us good, and it did. We watched a huge crack in the plate glass windows grow every time the wind blew. We had a bet that while we were staying at the hotel, that window would eventually blow out and kill at least one person. Things like that didn't seem to faze anyone there.

We met a group of people from Atlanta,

Georgia, and they inspired us to forge on regardless of what the lawyers had to say. As many as ten women arrived in Bucharest the same weekend as we did. Only one woman brought her husband to Romania while the other women were forced to leave their husbands at home to continue working and taking care of their other children. They were merely looking to build their families by adopting a Romanian orphan. They moved into a large apartment together and were to be a good source of information and moral support. We exchanged phone numbers and promised to keep in touch.

We had brought a walkman and a few choice cassette tapes from home, and it was the best thing we could have done. The music relaxed us and greatly enhanced our frame of mind. When I listened to Bonnie Raitt's song, "In The Nick of Time," I knew we just barely made it into that country to adopt in the nick of time. Like the woman in the song, I too was running out of time. When ever I listened to that particular song, tears would well up in my eyes, and I knew I would never again be able to listen to that song back home without recalling how it made me feel when our time was about to run out.

After we had a quick bite to eat we hurried back to our room to wait for our lawyer to call us. The waiting was unbearable as we were hoping that he wouldn't tell us to give up too. We didn't want to hear that again, because we were not going to give up. The tension made us ill. We got back down on our knees and started to pray again. We felt so abandoned there, and we were sick from crying so much. I couldn't ever remember feeling that sad and scared at the same time. It was probably because we had so much on the line. I thought that the next time in my life that we would be that sad would be at our parents' funerals. I wondered why God was putting us through such uncertainty that was causing us such anguish. What had we done to deserve such pain? I thought about all of the pain I had ever experienced in my life and realized that this was the worst. I thought that if I could just cut off my right arm to leave Romania with a baby, I would gladly have done it.

At 11 p.m. our lawyer finally called us and reassured us that he would straighten his staff out and they would help us find a baby. It all sounded so easy. (Could it be so easy?) We had cried and worried ourselves sick and our lawyer said he would fix everything. Well, that was what we needed to hear, and it did help us to sleep a little easier. We really needed to sleep. That was all those words were worth, one good nights sleep.

Sunday May 19th: We barely made it to breakfast before the restaurant closed at 11 a.m. It was not really worth rushing for - tea and rolls again. Already we were sick of it. As soon as breakfast was over, we were doomed to another day of torturous and endless nothing-to-do syndrome. Our American attorney forgot to tell us that his staff didn't work on the weekends. When we first arrived, we were ready to go to work on the adoption. No one told us how boring weekends were there, but we quickly found out. I hated being a shut in. I never played that role well. I needed to be accomplishing major multiple tasks periodically throughout the day. I was in the middle of who-the-hell-knows-where, doing absolutely nothing at all, and it was driving me insane. I decided to think about

61

all of the things that I had done with my life, and after I did that, I thought of all of the things that I could do with my life. Then I decided to think about the things in life that I really loved. That helped a lot until I thought about Sparkey, and I got real sad as I missed her more than anything in the world. My dog is my best friend. She would always listen to my troubles and she always let me cry on her. I missed the way she would always follow me around everywhere I went with her cute little waggy tail. She has such a distinct personality that I have grown to love, and now I missed her so much. Romania wouldn't be nearly so bad if Sparkey was here, I thought.

The reason weekends in Romania were so boring was because everything closed down, completely. When the town shuts down, I shut down because there was absolutely nothing to do. It was all very depressing, and not at all what we were accustomed to. We thought it might do us a world of good to socialize with some of the Americans we met in the hotel lobby. We knew that if they were as bored as we were, we could all help each other. However, listening to their stories made us feel uneasy. Some people had been there for months fighting the red tape. Listening to those couples made me realize that I had been fooling myself into thinking that we could accomplish an adoption there. Once we were settled we had to find a way to make it work.

At 8 p.m. Lili and Mario came to our hotel to talk to us again. They were still reluctant to help us with the adoption, as they were convinced that they would go to jail. They said they spoke with our lawyer but he didn't understand the fear that the Romanian people felt while assisting in the adoptions. Lili agreed to take us to Nicoresti on Tuesday to visit Julie, but it was understood that it was not intended to look for a baby. I was so discouraged with the operations of the firm that we hired, and I was beginning to doubt their legitimacy. They were very willing to promise us the world back in New York when they took our money, but when we needed them, they were doing nothing for us. We began to realize that it was up to us to be creative on how we were going to accomplish our goals. We spent endless hours devising plans and methods of overcoming the roadblocks, if only it was possible to do.

We confided in Lili and Mario that we needed to exchange American dollars into lei. We said that we would be willing to do it on the black market if they would help us. Before we knew it, we were off in Mario's little taxi heading to a seedier part of town. It was after 9 p.m. and we knew the American Consulate had a travelers advisory warning us not to be on the streets after dark. There we were, in the scariest place in the world, with $7,000 cash on us, in some dark alley just asking for trouble. Mario said in his broken English, "Give me money" and we thought, "All right, Mario. What money? The $100 we want to exchange or the $7,000 in our money belts that you are about to rob us of?" We were so scared we didn't know what to do. Finally Lili told us that it would be best for Mario to exchange the $100 for us. We handed over the money and watched this man we barely knew walk off into the dark shadows of the run down buildings where wild dogs were barking uncontrollably and half-naked-children where hitting each other with sticks. I thought at any moment we would be attacked by a band of thieves and robbed of everything.

Mario was gone for at least thirty minutes and during that time we sat in the cold. The only thing that broke the silence was the chattering of my teeth - not because of the dampness, but because of the fright. I said many prayers waiting for Mario to return. Beads of sweat were on my brow when out of nowhere Mario appeared. I didn't see any sign of an exchange. He looked very serious and without uttering a word, he hopped in the car and drove off. As we approached a better section of town, Mario pulled the car off the road and swung his arm over the back seat and looked at us, two scared little chicks. Mario smiled and said, "I got you 165, that is good you know." He proceeded to pull huge stacks of old dirty and smelly lei from under his shirt. When he handed it to us, we sighed with relief and thought how foolish we were to risk so much for so little. Later in the evening when we were getting ready for bed, Pat admitted to me that he thought it was thrilling to live on the edge like that. For me, I didn't need thrills like that. I could think of a lot of better things that we could be doing that were thrilling, yet safer and legal. It certainly did enhance our boring weekend where our only accomplishment had been preventing bedsores.

After the money exchange, it was difficult to go to bed and expect to be able to go to sleep as if what we had just done was no big deal. To me, it was a big deal, and the only other time in my life that I lived so close to the edge was when I was eighteen years old and lived in the South Pacific. I recalled having snorkeled in a shark pass where my only worry at the time was whether or not the tiny blue Damsel fish might get caught in my long brown hair. I fell to sleep dreaming of the carefree days in the South Pacific, where the warm sun relaxed my tanned body, and the ocean waves could mesmerize me for hours.

# Chapter 6
# **Fields**

---

Monday May 20th: Back home we couldn't wait for weekends to come. There were TGIF parties, happy hours, and nights out on the town. Somehow Americans came alive again after spending the work week in a comatose state. Unless of course, you were in the minority of those who enjoy going to work! In Romania, the opposite was true for us. Fridays became like Mondays, and Mondays like Fridays to us. Partly because everything – stores, shops, and businesses - were virtually closed on the weekends. The Romanians who worked for the American law firm we hired didn't work on the weekends, which forced us to become shut-ins. Mondays were the greatest thing to us while in Romania. It was like being released from jail. I never thought I would look forward to a Monday morning the way I did in Romania. When our alarm clock rang, I was out of bed as if it was on fire. For me, it was time to go to work, and that was why we were there. I was even eager to go to breakfast for my usual tea and rolls.

By 9 a.m. we found our way to the United States Embassy and there was a line a mile long of Americans who looked so tired and worn down from temporarily living there. Most of them had children and I was envious of them because they were on their way out and I was just starting the process. I felt sorry for them because it was so cold and it was raining, and many of the children were sick. I couldn't understand why everyone had to wait outside in the elements. When I looked into the eyes of some of the couples applying for their exit visas, they seemed almost hollow, and the looks on their faces said it all. Some offered advice to us, "Dig in your heels, get as tough as you possibly can, and don't give up." Once I had that wisdom, I wanted to get out there and find a baby. I had only been in that country one lousy weekend and I felt the tension building already. I wondered what I would be like one month from now if I was still there fighting.

Our one hour wait in line to get inside the U.S. Embassy passed rather quickly. We were fascinated, yet bewildered upon hearing some of the sagas from the other adopting Americans. The gentle morning breeze somehow managed to keep the American flag attached to the Embassy snapping. That scene tantalized us as we had no idea just how long the adoption process would take at the rate we were going. As I looked away from this banner, this symbol of America, I felt so lucky and fortunate to be an American. My eyes then fell upon a group of Romanians across the street who were in silent protest, with banners of their own. From what I could determine, those people had all been denied exit visas to America for one reason or another. I couldn't tell however, who had denied them the visa, whether it was "Bucharest" or "Washington." One sign read, "Washington says yes, why Romania says no?" Some wanted to reunite with existing families in the states, others simply were seeking the freedom that we on the other side of the street had often taken for granted.

We had to dig out our American passports

and show them to a Romanian guard before he
would open the gate for us. The U.S. Marine
that greeted us inside as we entered the
Embassy shared little in common with the
Romanian soldier outside except for his
youthful face. While both wore military
uniforms, they greatly differed in appearance.
The Marine was polished, while the Romanian
was drab with tarnished buttons and scuffed
boots. Both had guns, yet of different makes
and sizes.

Once we finally got inside the Embassy we
sat with a group of Americans doing the same
thing we were doing. In a way, it gave us
inspiration that if those folks could adopt,
we could too. We confirmed with the Consulate
officials that it was legal to continue with
the adoption pursuit, just as we thought. We
made our way back to the InterContinental
Hotel, marching quickly in the street that had
separated the two growing groups on opposite
sidewalks. We immediately contacted the
Romanian office manager of the American law
firm we hired. We wanted her to assign us a
new translator to help us adopt a baby. Lili
was a nice person whom we liked a lot, but she
lacked adoption experience and was scared to
death to help us. Somehow the office manager
talked us into giving Lili one more try. We
agreed to go with Lili to Nicoresti to visit
Julie in the morning. Depending on the
outcome of that trip, we would decide whether
or not to keep her, or to go with Bogdon.
Whoever Bogdon was, we only hoped that he was
better and more aggressive than Lili. Once
again we placed a call to the states to the
attorney we hired to voice our concerns about
their operation. He reassured us that if Lili
didn't work out, that by Wednesday, Bogdon
would take over for her. Our lawyer spoke

very highly of Bogdon and said he was very aggressive. Part of me was glad, but the other part of me didn't believe our lawyer. Pat and I spent the entire evening devising action plans in the event that they were needed.

We listened to the two cassette tapes that we brought with us over and over again as we hashed over every thinkable option regardless of whether or not it was feasible. By midnight, the same songs took on a different tone as the batteries began to fade with the night. Exhausted from the day, we too were fading.

At 2 a.m. we were awakened by an unfamiliar noise that resembled the howling wind. At first we couldn't tell where it was coming from. We determined that it was not coming from inside the room, but from outside. Once we were standing outside on the balcony, we realized that though the night was calm, the Romanian people were not. Thousands of people were protesting in Victory Square. Unbeknownst to us, that night marked the one year anniversary of the so-called free elections. The Romanian people were demonstrating the fact that the elections were anything but free. The bullet holes on our balcony were a constant reminder that at any given time, another revolution could take place. The droning sounds of so many chanting people made it extremely difficult for us to fall back to sleep. My mind was racing with so many thoughts, and I was unsure of what it would take to calm me. I felt wired and wanted to solve the world's problems. The peacefulness of snow gently falling in the dead of winter was what unclouded my mind enough for me to fall back to sleep.

Tuesday May 21st: Pat's watch alarm went

off promptly at 7 a.m. We talked briefly about the sounds of the night as we got ready for the day. After our usual breakfast of tea and rolls, Lili picked us up for our day trip into the country. She informed us that Mario's car was again in the repair shop, but she managed to find another driver, Ralu. It turns out that Ralu was Mario's partner in the taxi cab business. It didn't take us long to discover that when you ride in a Romanian taxi, you were embarking on a journey of a lifetime. We thought the New York City cabs were bad. In Romania, it was like riding a roller coaster without a seat belt. For some unknown reason, taxi drivers were compelled to drive with a great sense of urgency, as if they were taking an expectant woman to a hospital to deliver a baby. Taxi drivers didn't know how to drive slowly or safely. Every cab we rode in went extremely fast, and stopped very short. Each time we had minor whiplash, but that was considered the "norm" in Romania. It was probably best for passengers once they were in the back seat of a cab, to slouch down and close their eyes. There was very little safety for pedestrians, largely due to the taxi drivers. If we didn't feel safe in the car, we surely didn't feel safe walking on the sidewalks. Knowing that, we feared the long journey ahead of us with Ralu.

In America, Ralu could easily be a linebacker for the Buffalo Bills and be nicknamed Brutus. With his husky frame and unshaven face, Ralu could have instilled fear in you, but deep down he was nothing more than a gentle giant. He drove like he was in the Indy-500 but without the proper equipment, and of course we were on narrow roads that were designed for horse drawn carts and speeds

70

below 30 mph.

It was going to be a new experience for us. We found ourselves more often in the passing lane than in our own, passing all of the slow moving vehicles, such as carts, tractors, and trucks. Though fourth gear was broken in Ralu's car, it didn't stop him from driving over 100 kilometers per hour. The noise of the car was deafening, and there was a strong odor of fumes which was sickening. I felt it was worth it to endure if that would help us locate our baby. On several occasions I screamed as Ralu slammed on the brakes and swerved to avoid hitting a cow, or another car. I don't know how he did it, but we were never involved in any accidents.

We did however get a speeding ticket in a small peasant village on the outskirts of Buzau, about two hours north of Bucharest. (Can you believe it? Radar guns and speed traps in Eastern Europe. Just like home!) I wanted to strangle that three-hundred-pound brute and say, "You idiot, you deserve this ticket. If you don't get us all killed, it will be a miracle." Instead, I reached in my purse and pulled out a package of Kent cigarettes to give the police. The officers looked like the Gestapo. They threw the cigarettes to the ground and said, "Papers, I want your papers." Pat and I pulled out our passports, while Lili and Ralu presented their papers as they must have done so many times before. Lili told them we were tourists headed for the north country. They were so intimidating, like we had just committed a criminal offense, as they issued Ralu a speeding ticket. Pat offered to pay the fine, but Ralu insisted. It set him back 200 lei ($1.50). They have no point system or tracking methodologies in Romania. The police

71

instilled the fear of God into us and caused the inconvenience of taking over an hour to find the courthouse to pay for the ticket. As we waited in the car while Ralu paid the fine, I looked deep into the eyes of the people who lived in that village wondering if my baby would look like any of them. Lili would often point out the Gypsies to us, as if their brightly colored costumes didn't reveal their identity.

When we finally got back on the road, the weather cleared up and we were able to open the windows for "fresh" air. Actually, the air was never fresh, especially in the car as Lili and Ralu were chain smokers so the smoke and ashes constantly burned our eyes. I tried to enjoy the spectacular scenery that surrounded us in every direction. The poorly paved roads were all lined with trees. In the distance we could always see where a road was because of the rows of trees. Green vegetables and golden grains created colorful acres of fields. The lands were dotted with peasants that appeared to be engulfed by the vastness of the land. We never did come across any tractors or machinery that aided them with their labors. We watched village peasants till fields by hand and walk for miles with one little bucket to fetch the daily water. Women would sit along the road side with a sickle in one hand and a rope attached to a cow in the other. They wore layers of clothes, and almost every woman I saw had a scarf wrapped tightly around her head. The older women with their tanned and wrinkled faces all wore toothless smiles. Everyone looked so poor. Yet if we didn't know about the years of suffering and despair the people of Romania endured under the Ceausescu regime, we almost would have envied their simple life style. I remembered complaining about raking leaves at home, and in Romania, people work the land by hand. The fields seemed to go on forever, for as far as the eye could see. I vowed never again to complain about the yard work at home.

By that time, Pat and I had stopped looking at the speedometer, tuned out the squealing of the tires, and stopped back seat driving. We were going to put our lives in Gods hands, not Ralu's. While we were going through our infertility struggle, we had to remind ourselves daily that we had to trust in God and His ways. When we were planning our trip to Romania in search of our family, we felt that it was He who called us there. We had to trust Him. However, with each and every mile we journeyed, it was getting more and more difficult to keep our faith.

It was only a few miles outside of Buzau that I saw the Blessed Mother over my right shoulder. I took Pat's hand and I said, "I see Mary out the back window." Pat must have thought I was losing my mind, but she was there. Pat looked in back, but he couldn't see her. Every time I looked, there she was like an angel on my shoulder, or was it in fact my guardian angel? She was wearing a red dress and had both of her arms stretched out around us. She also had a crown of sparkling stars around her head. It was like the pictures I had seen, only this was so much better. I told Pat, "We are golden because Mother Mary is riding with us. I have a feeling that we are going to get our baby on this trip." Pat and I held hands and prayed to Mary all the way to Nicoresti.

We finally reached our destination around 2 p.m. We would have been there sooner if it were not for the speeding ticket and getting lost in the country. I knew we were in trouble when Ralu pulled off the road and asked Lili to get the map out. The two of them argued in Romanian for over ten minutes, occasionally lifting their heads from the map, and looked at the various road signs. We had traveled over 300 kilometers northeast of Bucharest, through some of the most fertile lands of Romania, to reach Nicoresti. The small village was surrounded by gently rolling hills and was located in the middle of Romania's finest wine country. I was excited to finally meet Julie, the woman from Syracuse who had inspired us to adopt from Romania.

As we passed the orphanage where Julie worked and headed towards her apartment building, the words and images of her letters flashed back to me. The visions that I had while reading her letters were becoming less surrealistic and frightfully real. As soon as we got out of the car we were quickly surrounded by a group of children that came out of the apartment building. As I said, "Buna ziua," which means hello, they all smiled and giggled a warm hello in return. That was the first time I spoke Romanian and it felt so good to receive such a genuine response.

We finally met Julie, and I was able to give her a letter that I hand carried from her father along with a small care package from home. I wanted to convey to Julie how deeply she had touched our hearts and inspired us to forge on with an idea that we could adopt from Romania. I didn't even know Julie, yet I was planning to name my first child after her. I hoped that she didn't think I was a lunatic. Julie introduced us to some of the other volunteers. They could only stay a few moments though. Time enough for a quick smoke and a cup of coffee before going back to the orphanage. While I couldn't recall any names, their faces still remain with me. They had come from all over the world; Ireland, Canada, Britain, America, and Bucharest, to give of themselves to the forgotten children of Romania. Seeing the sacrifices that they had to endure for the sake of the children reaffirmed our faith in mankind.

Pat wanted to walk through her orphanage, but Lili thought that after talking to Julie, we should go to several orphanages to try to find a baby. For me, getting a baby and going home was my only priority. After hearing what other adopting couples had gone through, along with being faced with the doors closing, it had to be our only priority. We chose not to question Lili's change of heart in helping us locate a baby on the trip. We said our good-byes as we dropped Julie off at the orphanage. Julie had told us earlier that there were orphanages located in the cities of Galati and Braila, both of which were a short drive south of Nicoresti. She knew of some American volunteers that worked in those orphanages and gave us their names. At that point, we took all the help that we could get.

By the time we reached Galati, it was well after 4 p.m. Located near the Soviet border, Galati is a major river port on the Danube River, and is the principal shipbuilding center for Romania. The work day was winding down and the streets were full of people whose callous and hard lives showed in their faces. We had to stop a number of times and ask for directions to the orphanage. However, when we finally arrived, we were coldly told that the directoress had left for the day. We felt like Dorothy in the "Wizard of Oz." We had traveled so far only to be told that the person who could help us was gone, and we too should go home! We decided to stay over night and return to the orphanage in the morning.

We drove to the city of Braila to locate Julie's friends who worked in the nearby orphanages. We checked into the Hotel Belvedere where they apparently lived. As we walked into the lobby, I began to panic, wondering how much the hotel would cost us. The lobby was enormous and everywhere I looked I saw marble pillars, and spiral stair cases with hand made rugs. Lili told me we were in trouble because they wouldn't accept credit cards and therefore we would have to pay cash for our room, Lili's room, and Ralu's room. Lili looked really scared when she told me how much we would have to pay. The total was 400 lei for theirs and 1,700 for ours. I wondered if that was the key deposit, but it was the cost of the room. (1,700 lei = $10.30) I know my mouth hung open and Lili thought it was too much money. After all, her room cost $1.20. Our room rate was higher because of the foreigner's tax that we were forced to pay. Romanians were excluded from that tax but all other tourists were required to pay higher prices for almost everything.

Our rooms were on the third floor and we had a beautiful view of the Danube River. I had always dreamed of seeing the Danube, and there I was. There were no lights in the halls leading to our rooms and I was afraid walking in pitch darkness. Our room had only one 25-watt light bulb, no lock on the door, and the chair that Pat propped against it didn't give me much reassurance. The bathroom window, which gave us another view of the Danube, and the hotel terrace, remained permanently open due to its broken window frame. The bathroom was clean; however there

76

was no soap and no toilet paper. There was
only one small hand towel that was worn so
thin that I could see right through it. We
later discovered there was no hot water. So
why have soap and nice towels? No one would
be using them anyway.

Our dining experience in the hotel
restaurant made up for the shortcomings of the
room. The atmosphere was exquisite, even
though most of the tables were empty. The
main dining room was spacious and airy with
twenty foot ceilings. Three of the four walls
were plate glass windows overlooking the murky
brown Danube River. A young and beautiful
waitress asked us if we would like to eat
"meat" for dinner. Lili told her yes and to
also bring the hotel's finest wine. Lili was
eager to celebrate her name's day, which was
the equivalent to our birthday celebrations.
Her given name was Elena and she therefore
wanted to commemorate the feast day of Saint
Elena. Lili was a nickname she acquired as a
child. The evening was a bit awkward because
we really didn't know them and though Lili did
speak good English, Ralu didn't know one word
of English. Throughout the evening we would
casually glance at each other, nod and smile.
For me, it was uncomfortable, but he was the
driver and we needed him as much as he needed
the $20 per day he was charging us. Thank God
we had Lili to translate.

Lili did a great job ordering the wine.
It was by far the best wine I had ever tasted
in my life, and it only cost 250 lei per
bottle ($1.50). The meal truly complimented
the wine. That was to be our first authentic
Romanian dish. Our meat was spiced pork along
with french fries, bottled drinks, coffee, and
desert. The total bill for the four of us
including the wine cost only $2.42. The meal

77

was exactly what I needed, because it took the edge off of the tension I felt.

The time during dinner gave us the opportunity to get to know Lili a little better. She told us that she had graduated from Bucharest University and worked as an architect designing, of all things, railroad buildings. We learned that she was an only child, and though her parents were still alive, she lived with her grandmother in a small apartment. Even though she enjoyed her work, her dream was to become a travel guide. Since she spoke and understood English well, Lili would be perfect for tours to Romania's many beautiful sites. Along with the Black Sea resorts, the Transylvania and Carpathian Mountain regions, there are the many beautiful monasteries that are scattered throughout Romania that are visited by tourists.

Later that evening we located the American women who volunteered their time in the Braila orphanages. It was nice to talk with other Americans, whether or not they would be able to help us. One woman was very cold to us when she learned that we were there for adoption purposes. It was her opinion that it was not right for Americans to be adopting the orphans. I personally thought she had no concept of the sacrifices the adopting couples were making by attempting to rectify the problem of the overabundance of abandoned and orphaned children. She did make one point: Romania does to its children what Americans do to their elderly. We both put them in "homes" and often forget about them.

We met a second volunteer who was more amicable and sympathetic to our cause. She was willing to help us in any way she could. She told us that there were many young, healthy, and beautiful infants in the orphanage in Braila and many of them were adoptable. The problem was that the directoress of that orphanage was corrupt and we were warned that she would need a big cash bribe. We had no idea what "big bribe" meant. Only a few hours earlier in the day, Lili told us that our hotel rooms would be expensive and her room cost under two dollars. She again cautioned us that the directoress was wicked to deal with. It would be a very difficult process, but we thought it would be worth it and asked Lili to help us. Lili however was reluctant to bribe the orphanage directoress. We tried to reason with Lili all night, but she was set in her beliefs and was not going to risk any possible conflict with a vicious directoress.

Lili did say that she would take us to Galati first thing in the morning to try to find a baby there as we had heard from the American volunteers many favorable reports about how nice the orphanage was, and that the directoress was a fair and honest person. We started to feel as if we actually were living in the land of Oz. Was the directoress going to be a good witch or a bad witch? Pat would joke that we were about to meet the wicked witch of the east! We had talked to many couples who had dealt first-hand with those people. They told us that the fact that some orphanage employees had to be paid bribes to do their job was not the main thing that upset them. It was witnessing their lack of compassion and their attitude that the children, especially the handicapped, were regarded as disposable and not deserving of love and basic human care. Although it was true that most orphanages were understaffed and lacked many supplies, human kindness and compassion cost nothing.

I was angry with Lili that she wouldn't "toss a bribe" in Braila. It was not that we wanted to do that but we decided that while we were in Romania we would play their games by their rules to get children out of the orphanages. The thought of confronting a wicked directoress and paying her off to adopt a child really didn't sit well with me, but I knew that it might be necessary, and I was willing to do it. Often I would turn to Pat and say, "Can you believe what we are saying?" Pat would hold his head in his hands and say, "When the time is right, we will do the right thing."

We wanted to walk along the river before the sun set but we were warned that bands of Gypsy boys circled around tourists and beat them with sticks and robbed them before throwing them into the Danube. We were also advised not to go near any stray dogs because they were all wild, and would just as soon take off our arm if we tried to feed them. Because of that we decided to retreat back to the room where we could lock ourselves in and feel somewhat safe. There was an old short-wave radio next to the bed. Pat tried to tune in a station, perhaps one from Russia since we were so close, but the air waves were silent. Pat double checked to make sure our barricade chair lock was still secure. We slept with one eye open, wearing our clothes with our money belts on. It was by far the worst night's sleep I ever had. We listened to wild dogs howl all night, and I cried myself to sleep thinking about Sparkey, wondering if she was thinking of me.

Since we had not anticipated staying overnight, none of us had a change of clothes or any of the usual grooming aids. I knew we all looked and felt pretty haggard when we met in the lobby in the morning. Breakfast was a treat, consisting of omelets, tea, rolls, and Coke, costing only 300 lei for the four of us ($1.80). I had butterflies in my stomach and couldn't wait to hit the road as I was anxious to get to Galati. After all, this could be the day that I met my child.

Once we were in the car, I was even more anxious because I had forgotten just how bad Ralu's driving was. The farther east we drove, the worse the roads became. At one point in the road, we came upon a washed out bridge. Instead of backing up and turning around, we drove across the river bed on top of two by fours that had been laid down in the shallow water. Once again I looked over my right shoulder and there was Mother Mary with her arms stretched out around us. This time she wore blue and white. I squeezed Pat's hand as I told him Mary was still with us and I felt confident that we were going to have luck in Galati. (Why else would I be able to see The Blessed Mother of God? This had to be the ultimate sign.) Pat and I prayed the entire thirty-minute trip and felt emotionally exhausted by the time we approached the orphanage.

As we walked towards the building I saw on both sides of me fields of beautiful children. I wanted to run up to them and take as many as I could in my arms and run with them. They were all so adorable as each and every child stopped playing to watch us pass by. I wondered if they were hoping that we would take them home. I know I certainly wanted to, if only I could. I was trembling inside, as so many wild thoughts were whirling through my mind. Pat and I held each other as we fought back tears and blessed ourselves as we walked up the cascade of cement stairs. There were no words to explain what it was like walking down the cold, dark corridor looking past the rooms where we knew children played, on our way to the director's office.

Once we found her office we walked in and saw several women wearing white coats. Lili began to speak to them while Pat and I tried to hide our fear. After words were exchanged, Lili translated to us that there were no adoptable children in the orphanage. I nearly fainted as I felt all of the blood drain from my head. I sobbed into Pat's chest in disbelief. There were over three hundred children there, and I couldn't accept that all of them were unadoptable. We were told that many birth parents leave their children for safe keeping until they can afford to take them. The reality was that quite often the parents would never return, and the poor children spend their entire lives institutionalized. I couldn't understand how people could take their children and put them in an orphanage for safe-keeping.

The orphanage employees wore heavy overcoats and their breath could be seen when they talked. That meant to us that the buildings didn't have proper heat. The children didn't get any food; they only got broth. Many of the children slept in metal cages until they were five years old. Their beds were soaked in urine; they had no diapers, and they rarely got baths. There was no medicine if they got sick. We recalled the television show "20|20" that first shocked the world with horrible scenes depicting the deplorable conditions in Romania's orphanages. Julie's letters also revealed to us the poor state of the facilities that she worked in.

My mind raced on the car trip home. I thought about everything under the sun. I thought about our friends Becky and Steve and I wondered what they would have said to us at a time like that. I wanted to scream from all of the evil thoughts I had. How could our prayers not be answered? How could God let us down? Would we be going home without a child? I resented everyone that I knew who could get pregnant. I wondered if Mary was still with us. Every time I looked over my right shoulder I could see her. I couldn't figure out why. Why would Holy Mary be with me after my dreams were just crushed?

In the distance I saw a huge field of wild storks. I fantasized that many of those storks would deliver some of Romania's orphaned children to good homes; that just one stork from that flock would deliver a baby to me. The journey back to Bucharest took close to four hours, and during that time we never spoke a word. Ralu left us at our hotel, and once Pat and I were in our room, we held each other and cried uncontrollably. We got down on our knees and began to pray. I couldn't ever remember praying as hard as we did on that day.

Before going out for an early dinner, we called some of the friends we made from Atlanta when we first arrived in Bucharest. They encouraged us to go to the Commission to request the name of a handicapped child. They said that the Commission would only give out handicapped children's names. The adoption Commission had been created by the Romanian government to gain control and regulate the adoption process. They were supposed to have on file a list of children in orphanages throughout the entire country who were adoptable. In reality, much of their information was inaccurate and many feel that the Commission was more of a hindrance than anything else. We spoke with many couples who, after receiving a name from the Commission, traveled great distances, only to find that the child didn't exist or had already been adopted months ago.

Like most first-time parents to be, we wanted a healthy infant, but I began to realize that it was not going to happen. If we wanted a family, we would have to take an older child, or a handicapped child. The more we talked about it, the more comfortable we became with the idea that we would be bringing home a child that was simply a little different than what our families were expecting. We hurried to the Commission to request the name of an adoptable child but they wouldn't see us. It was four o'clock and they were getting ready to leave for the day. I pleaded with the lady in charge that I only wanted one name. She questioned why I would want a retarded child. As a tear welled up in my eye I said, "Because I want a family." Her sinister smile went blank as she told me to return in the morning at 8 a.m. and she would then grant me my wish.

During the afternoon Lili gave us a walking tour of Victory Square. It was a bit eerie knowing that was the place where so many people had gathered just a few days earlier to protest. There were still a few demonstrators left and I wanted to take a picture of them. Lili warned me that I could be arrested for taking photographs in the square. Lili also advised me not to stand on the street because that too was against the law. Loitering was not something that you do in Romania, for it was interpreted as a sign that you were up to something. She, along with the entire population, must have been programmed to believe that someone was always watching you and this intimidation forced you to go about your business. Lili also explained that women who smoke on the streets were thought to be prostitutes, and therefore were arrested. The more she told me, the more I began to understand how difficult it must be to live in Romania. I always took my United States citizenship for granted until that day. America has its share of crazy laws and problems. However, we would never know what it must be like to live in a place where you were forced to keep your thoughts to yourself.

Pat and I returned to our hotel room and prepared another camper meal for dinner. They were easy to make; just boil some water in the hot pot that we brought, and mix it in the pouch. It tasted pretty good for freeze-dried food, and I was grateful to have it. After our meal, we reflected on our day, and realized that we were becoming exhausted from the circumstances that we were being faced with. Pat started smoking again for the first time in over seven years. I showed no emotion as he lit up each and every cigarette, hoping he would eventually be able to quit. I was very homesick, and found myself looking through things in my suitcase because it reminded me of home. It was then that I was surprised by a card from Becky, my friend from Syracuse, in my suitcase. The card didn't say much, but it had a lot of love in it. I must have read it over a thousand times. I found a bag of chocolates that I brought with me to give as a "gift." I decided that I needed a gift, and ate the whole bag.

We discussed how difficult it must be to live in a country where people can't have conversations in private without another set of mysterious ears listening in. We had heard that Romania was a place where half of the people were spying on the other half. In fact, we were told that the InterContinental Hotel was, and perhaps still is, a headquarters for the secret police with rooms filled with listening devices. Initially, I was not convinced that our room was "bugged," but as time went on, I was sure that the walls had ears.

The first incident occurred when we had a discussion about how dirty our drapes were. The once beautiful white material had not seen a cleaning in quite some time. The next day we had new drapes. The second episode took place after we discussed how the maid was not leaving Swiss chocolates on our pillows like the other hotel guests received because she was eating them. The next evening gold coins filled with Swiss chocolate magically appeared on our pillows. After several days of Pat and I griping over sharing a bath towel, we stood in the center of the room and shouted to the ceiling, "It sure would be nice to have more than one towel." We were not surprised when we started to receive all the towels that we needed. It was possible that those happenings were just coincidental, but they were far from isolated incidences. Pat and I became selective in what we wanted who-knows-who to hear.

We decided to phone the Romanian office manager from the American law firm that we were working with to review our situation. She told us that one of the lawyers from the firm had just arrived in Bucharest for some other business. We called him that night to voice our concerns with his firm. We again relayed our displeasure with Lili and told him the trip in the country was unsatisfactory. He promised us that he would try to find us another guide. In the meantime, he told us that he would meet us at the Commission in the morning. We were pleased that he would meet us there because we hoped that maybe with his representation we would be successful using the Commission.

While we arrived promptly at the agreed upon hour outside the Commission entrance, our lawyer showed up two hours late. During our idle time, we would impolitely stare at the people entering the gateway into the courtyard that led to various government buildings. Our inquisitive stares were reflected back to us from all who passed us by. Lili pointed out to us that Americans were easily identified, not necessarily by the way we dressed, but more because of our mannerisms. Americans tended to display an uneasiness about themselves. Lili said that we examined everything around us whether it was a building, a store front, or a group of people. While those actions may seem typical of any tourist in a foreign country, they contrasted sharply with the mannerisms of a Romanian. The Romanian people had been programmed not to talk to strangers, especially foreigners and to keep to themselves. These mannerisms, although changing, had been a result of the years of living in a society where all actions were strictly controlled.

We tried to imagine what other reasons people had for coming to this place surrounded by a thick cement barrier. How many of these people were like us, here to adopt and to beg the Commission for a name? What other reasons would draw people to such a place? We noticed that there was a Romanian family that had been waiting outside the gate for nearly as long as we had. The family had spanned three generations. Lili overheard them say that they were applying for larger living accommodations in a state dwelling. There was an adorable child with them who past the time away playing hopscotch on the sidewalk. I approached her with a package of Beechnut gum in my outstretched hand saying, "Guma." Delighted, the child ran to me, for the treasure. I don't know why I was so compelled to take that child's picture. I only knew that I had to have it. She proudly displayed her package of gum as a trophy to all who passed by. I received so much gratification from that child that I would often distribute packs of gum to children I would see on the streets.

Eventually our lawyer arrived and the Commission officials saw us. Once Pat and I were called into "the room" to get the name of a child, we found a much different picture than what we were expecting. The board seemed to examine us from head to toe as we scurried past them to take our seats. Though I tried to remain focused on our chairs, I casually glanced at their expressionless faces. We were seated in the center of a room surrounded by the officials who sat on an elevated platform. It was very intimidating because everyone looked down on us, as if they were God's chosen people on judgment day.

A young Romanian woman sat with us and acted as an interpreter. She carefully paged through our dossier package containing our homestudy which revealed our financial worth. She asked us questions like why would we want to adopt a sick or handicapped child? Pat and I reached down deep into our souls to answer those questions which seemed to last forever. Finally, we were told that we could have a one-year-old blind baby girl. I looked at Pat in disbelief as blindness was one thing we never discussed and neither of us knew what to say. Apparently saying nothing was the right thing to do. A few moments later we were told that there was a two-month-old baby boy named Auriel, and if we wanted him, he was ours. I asked what the handicap was and they replied, "Problems at birth." God only knows what that meant, but we said okay instantly. I was excited to hurry up and get him, but nothing in Romania moves that fast. Once we were given the name, we had to wait in their waiting room for over four hours to get the special Commission paper with its special stamp and seal, which enabled us to see Auriel.

Instead of waiting for the special paper, we ate lunch with our lawyer. This allowed us to further explain that even though we had the name of a child, we still insisted on a new interpreter. We knew we were making many demands on his law firm, but that was why we hired them. We were unsure of the firm's legitimacy, and doubted every word they told us. They were placating us just to get us off of their backs, and I hated the game they were playing with us. Considering what we paid for their services, we expected better treatment from them. Pat and I realized that we were on our own and it was up to us to make our adoption work. It was apparent to us that our attorney had no intention of replacing Lili. Maybe he had no one to replace her with, or maybe he just didn't care about us as clients. After all, he had our money, and we knew there were no guarantees with a Romanian adoption using his firm. I was certain that his firm misrepresented itself to us, and there we were, stuck between a rock and a hard place, paying the ultimate price.

Once we received the official Commission paperwork, we rushed to Bucharest Orphanage

Number One to see Auriel. I was very anxious as I had no idea what we were about to encounter. I had uneasy feelings about walking into orphanages after our experiences in Galati. I prayed our experience in Bucharest would be better. The dimly lit office room that we first walked into was damp and depressing. The calendar that hung on the wall was two years old. There was a yellow ceramic furnace against one wall, and I stood next to it for warmth.

In the center of the room sat a young woman, wearing her winter coat, working behind an old dirty metal desk. Her stern face never cracked a smile as she greeted us. While reviewing our paper work, she began screaming in Romanian to Lili. The hair on the back of my neck stood straight up when Lili turned to me and said there was a problem. "What now?" I said in disgust. The clerk responded, "There is nothing wrong with Auriel and therefore you can't have him because only handicapped children are currently being adopted through the Commission, and if Auriel is not handicapped, then you can't have him." I was elated inside that he was healthy, but I was burning mad that finally I had the endorsement of the Romanian Commission, and that clerk was going to stand in my way and deny me Auriel. I pointed my finger at her and told Lili to translate word for word: "Are you calling the officials on the Commission board liars? Because if you are, then you will have to tell them so. They declared Auriel handicapped because he had problems at birth, and I believe them." After saying that, I pulled a gift out of my bag and slid it across her desk. Immediately she smirked as she announced that a gift was not necessary. Yet her inquisitive eyes

90

frequently glanced at the bag filled with lace underwear, jewelry, and chocolates. It appeared that the gift on her desk caused her personality to change. Her stone face had a smile scratched on it as she went to her files which consisted of an old shoe box filled with index cards. She proclaimed that there was no birth certificate for Auriel in the shoe box. The clerk told us that we would have less paperwork to do if Auriel was truly abandoned. With no birth certificate, there were no birth parents. Therefore, we could expedite the adoption proceedings.

Though our hearts were quietly rejoicing, we were disappointed to learn that the orphanage director had left for the day and that we couldn't see Auriel until the next day. I really wanted to see him, but there was no way possible without risking losing him to the system. We hung our heads low and left, half disappointed, half elated. I was beginning to understand the adoption game that we were playing. One minute you were on cloud nine, and the very next minute your spirits were crushed. One thing was certain, the game we played was for fighters only. I found that we were required to fight for every little thing. Already I was tired of fighting.

We were getting low on lei as the trip in the country had consumed the $100 we converted in the dark alley. I was not anxious to return to that dark alley to exchange money so we gave Mario $100 to exchange for us. Some people said we were stupid to trust Mario like that but it was worth the risk to me because we stood to lose a whole lot more by exchanging the money ourselves. Mario became a friend to us and we trusted him completely. He did come through for us with a decent exchange rate at 165.

Mario and Lili felt that we needed to get away from the rat race of the city and relax instead of returning to our room and fretting over what the next day would bring. We went to a lake in a nearby park for some peace and relaxation. It was exactly what we needed. We needed a rest from the countless hurdles we were constantly required to jump. It was hard not to think about Auriel because I couldn't help but wonder what he looked like. I envisioned him playing ball in the back yard with Pat and running after Sparkey. I imagined myself baking cookies for him and quietly reading books to him as he sat on my lap. I could see him in the crib at home and calling me "mama." Already I was in love with this child and I had not yet even seen him, but I just had a feeling he was ours. Lili warned me not to think about him because things could go wrong. I couldn't see how. After all we had a Commission slip. He was ours.

The park was located approximately twenty miles outside of the city and was considered to be the largest forest in Bucharest. The weather was splendid, because it didn't rain. We sat at rusty tables outside under a ragged gray canopy tent. We drank wine and nibbled on cucumbers, bread, and cheese as we listened to a small lounge style band that was set up on the patio. Although the place was practically empty, the musicians performed with much emotion. Their repertoire ranged from traditional Romanian ballads and American standards to pre-1970's contemporary hits. Although rock and roll music was over thirty years old, it was still a new sound to many Romanians. When the band played Louis Armstrong's version of "Mack the Knife," Lili knew the words better than we did! She

92

reveled in singing along with the band, especially songs that came from America.

I fed cheese to a mangy dog who sat beside my chair. For some reason that pooch reminded me of my dog and I couldn't help myself from wondering if Sparkey was okay. It felt great to be outdoors, away from the noise and smell of the city. From across the marshy waters, I heard my first wild cuckoo bird. Lili told me that those birds abandon their young at birth. Pat and I talked about buying a cuckoo clock in Switzerland for Auriel on our way home. As we walked around the lake we came upon a festive Gypsy houseboat filled with people dressed in a variety of bright-colored costumes, dancing to traditional Romanian folk music. They looked as if they didn't have a worry in the world.

I was actually feeling paranoid about walking around in that park with $7,000 cash on us and decided to call it a day. Knowing we had a long drive home, Lili directed me to the restroom which was nothing more than an out-house. I walked inside, and it was so dark that I couldn't even see where the toilet was. When I looked down, I strained my eyes to see two foot prints covered with human excrement. I ran out gasping for air and asked Mario to drive us home as fast as he could. Just then a huge deer jumped out in front of us and I couldn't believe my eyes. It was astonishing to see such incredible beauty and horrid filth within minutes of each other. It was becoming evident that with every day we stayed in that country, we would be subjected to many diverse things. We would have to take the good with the bad.

It was difficult for us to get to sleep that night because we couldn't stop wondering about Auriel. We prayed all night that the adoption would work for us. We had been in Romania a week and we felt exhausted from the emotional roller coaster we had been riding. I wondered what we would do if we were unable to adopt Auriel. With time running out, we could only continue to put our faith in God that it would work for us.

The U.S. Embassy in Bucharest, Romania.

This shrine was erected at the University Center in
remembrance of the people who lost their lives during
the revolution of 1989.

Victoria Street in Bucharest. The tall apartment building
on the left is the apartment Robin and Dave lived in.

This woman is selling fresh berries in Sinaia, Romania.

Predeal is the highest town in Romania, rising at 3,412 feet in elevation. The air was fresh and the scenery spectacular.

A woman selling a lace tablecloth for $6.00.

This women is selling flowers in the center of the city, Bucharest, Romania. This was a very common sight.

This woman is standing next to a câpitâ (pronounced cupeepza, known as a haystack). It will be used to feed the animals during the winter. Southern Brasov, Romania

# Chapter 7
# Auriel

---

Friday May 24th: After our tea and rolls, Mario and Lili picked us up at the hotel to take us to Bucharest Orphanage Number One. Once again Pat and I were a bundle of nerves as we walked into the orphanage. We tried to memorize every detail of the orphanage from the shady trees outside to the chipped white walls inside, so that we could someday tell Auriel all about it. We saw a British nurse walking with a young child. When she said, "Hello," I ran up to her and quickly showed her my Commission paper with Auriel's name and asked her if she knew him. She glanced at it briefly and her eyes twinkled and her round face had a big smile stretched over it. She said, "Auriel is my all-time favorite child, and he is perfectly normal and healthy. You are so lucky to get him." Tears filled my eyes as I thanked her sincerely. She directed me down a long narrow hall to the orphanage director's office.

A female doctor approached us and took us by the hand. Her tattered dress was hidden beneath her stained white lab coat. The gray locks of her hair wisped at the edge of her collar as we walked together, hand in hand, like Romanian women often did. Her petite and tired face wrinkled as she repeated, "Santa Maria" and occasionally blessed herself. Her gibberish was full of enthusiasm and emotion. I wished I knew what her words meant; I somehow knew what she felt. She was probably glad that we were adopting Auriel. He was one of the lucky children to leave the orphanage. The anticipation was building with each and every step we took. I felt as if I had cement blocks attached to my feet, yet my body was responding like a toy that was wound too tight. I simply couldn't wait to see our baby boy. We eventually walked through five buildings and up seven flights of stairs. She led us into a bright and airy room that was clean and warm, and pointed to a small white metal crib and she said, "Auriel."

When I looked at him it was love at first sight. I began crying hysterically as he was the most beautiful baby in the world. The doctor held me and cried too. She was genuinely happy for us. The doctor was blessing us and praying over us, and by that time, Pat was crying too. We couldn't believe that our dreams were finally coming true. Auriel was a gift from God and we felt truly blessed. The doctor picked him up and immediately tore his wet clothes off to show me he was normal. She also showed me his penis. Maybe she didn't know that I already knew he was a boy. The doctor put him into my arms and it felt like heaven. He was a heavy little chunk and much older than two months. I didn't care. He was strong and alert and he appeared to be a normal child, craving the love that we couldn't wait to give him. For over two hours, Auriel was mine to cherish. That child had so much affection poured into him during the short time we had with him. Another British nurse came by to tell us that she had always given Auriel special treatment. She told me that he was underweight and malnourished when he was abandoned at birth. No one really wanted or expected him to live.

They put him in a room and closed the door and forgot about him until this nurse found him and nurtured him. She told me that he was listed as a handicapped child because he was Gypsy. To me, he looked Italian, like Pat, and we decided to call him Daniel Joseph.

The Social Assistant from the orphanage told us it was time to go, so as I handed Auriel back, I gently kissed his tiny bald head and told him I would be back for him as soon as I could. I was anxious to start the paper work so Auriel could be with us in our hotel instead of the orphanage. We were off to locate Auriel's birth certificate. It was essential to obtain it in order for us to complete the adoption process.

Mario was waiting for us as we all piled into the car. The Social Assistant directed us to a nearby maternity hospital where Auriel was thought to have been abandoned. Lili and the Social Assistant went inside the hospital, leaving me and Pat waiting with Mario in the car. We prayed like mad that the adoption would work out for us, but we were painfully mistaken. Lili and the Social Assistant returned with disappointing news. We learned that the hospital didn't have the birth certificate, the birth parents had it. Apparently Auriel had a mother and a father, not married, and we had to approach them to get their consent for the adoption.

Nearing the endless rows of government apartment blocks, Mario parked the car in front of the tall gray building where Auriel's birth parents resided. As Lili and the Social Assistant quickly disappeared into the mammoth cement structure, visions of their confrontation raced through my mind. What did the couple look like? As Pat and I patiently waited in the car, the buzzing of Mario's radio, and the drops of rain that danced on the car, distracted our wild and crazy thoughts. We agonized for over thirty minutes until we caught a glimpse of Lili and the Social Assistant walking towards the car. I could tell from the expression on their faces that there was trouble. Reluctantly and sorrowfully, Lili told us the birth parents wanted to keep their son. Lili said they fought a useless battle with them trying to convince them that they were doing the right thing by letting us adopt their boy. Considering the fact that they had not seen their child since they abandoned him over four months ago, it was evident that Auriel would be much better off with us. Auriel's mother had two other children and was pregnant again. Obviously, they were in no financial condition to raise four children, as they were barely making it.

The Social Assistant was sympathetic to me as I was sobbing uncontrollably. She touched my face and said, "I gave them the weekend to decide. By Monday, Auriel could be yours. Keep your fingers crossed and keep these flowers for good luck." She handed me the red carnations that she had brought with her that day. I held the flowers to my face. We appreciated all the Social Assistant tried to do for us. We especially liked the plan she developed by asking Auriel's birth parents to use the upcoming weekend to make their final decision. There was only a very small thread of hope left, yet we desperately clung to it.

When Lili dropped us off at the hotel, I knew we were in for a rough weekend. I felt as if I were dangling from the Empire State Building by a rope that was breaking. I thought about my friend from home who was also in Romania adopting. I became obsessed with finding and calling Maria. In an act of desperation, Pat and I immediately went to the United States Embassy in an attempt to try to locate her through them. Upon entering the country, we were required to register our names, addresses, and phone numbers with the Embassy. Within an hour I was on the phone with Maria. She already had her baby and was on her way home. I was in shock that her lawyer was so efficient, and ours was so unorganized. I couldn't remember what I said to Maria that day on the phone. I only recalled how desperate, sad, and tired I was. Maria offered to ask her lawyer to help us, but she warned us that her legal fees would be $5,000. After I talked to Maria I cried nonstop for hours. I couldn't remember ever feeling so confused, so despondent and low. I went out on the balcony and thought about spending another miserable weekend in the hotel room, staring out the window, knowing our time was running out, and still we had no child. We were going nowhere fast. I quickly left the noisy balcony and retreated to our quiet room. As I closed the glass door behind me, I left my wicked thoughts outside to be washed away by the drizzling rain.

We talked a lot about how we were lucky to have each other. Who'd care if we went home without a baby? Somehow we would get over it. We talked about buying that vacation home, but we remembered that we had just spent all of our money on our adoption. The more I thought about giving up, the angrier I became. I was sick and tired of being disgusted all of the time. I decided to do something about it. I was going to stop being weighted down with negative thoughts. We were going to fight like mad. We would devise 101 action plans on how to get a baby and get out of Romania before the doors closed. I was sick of crying - I was sick of feeling weak - I needed to get tough. There was one thing that I was sure of and that was that only the tough survive, and I was planning to be one of them. If we couldn't get a baby out in time, then at least we would give it a good fight. There was no point in making myself sick with thoughts on giving up. I wouldn't give up!

We ate our dinner in the hotel restaurant thinking that we needed to treat ourselves special. The meal was excellent, if only I knew what it was. I ordered a veal dish, but I somehow doubt I got veal. There were three pieces of meat, one was a knee joint, patella and all. In any event the change of scenery did us both good. We sampled the Romanian beer and thought that would jolly our spirits up a bit. In the restaurant a Beatles song played on the canned music system that passed for a radio. Pat perked right up and sang along really loud. At first I was embarrassed, and I told Pat to hush up. Then I thought, who really cares? Certainly not me. "Sing your heart out Pat," and with that, I joined in on a few lines myself. Pat was right, that we needed to do things that made us happy. It was hard to do but we found that it was the little things that we enjoyed the most.

When we returned to our room I pulled a package of Pringle potato chips out of the suitcase. We had just one diet Sprite and we made a little party out of it. Once we were in the right frame of mind, we devised different ways to adopt a baby. It was important for us that whatever we did, that it was the "right" thing. We wanted to make sure that it would be something that we could live with. We then noticed that we started to lose sight of what was actually "right" and what was actually "wrong." We did agree that we would do whatever it took to get Auriel out of the orphanage. If we needed to bribe people to do it, then we were prepared to do that. After all, it was poor little Auriel who was abandoned. He was the one who was stuck in the orphanage. If his parents wanted him, then they should take him home with them. Either way, Auriel was our first concern. We agonized over the decision as to whether or not to hire Maria's lawyer, but we knew that if all else failed with Auriel, we would have that to fall back on. We were not sure that her lawyer was legitimate. We were painfully aware of the stories about the baby selling from the "60 Minutes" television broadcast.

Saturday May 25th: When Saturday morning arrived, it was as if my guardian angel had told me during the night that Maria's lawyer was going to be an answer to our prayers. I remembered a story I heard in church as a child. The story was about a man who prayed to God to save him from a flood. A policeman warned the man to evacuate his home because the flood was inevitably coming. The man exclaimed, "God will save me" and with those words, the policeman left. The next day torrential rains flooded the area, and firemen went to get this man to evacuate his home. The man wouldn't leave with them because he held onto his belief that God would save him. A few hours later, the flood waters caused the man to sit on his roof top. A helicopter flew over and dangled a rope for the man to climb to safety, but the man said, "No thank you, God will save me" and the helicopter flew away. Soon thereafter, the man drowned. When he met God in heaven he asked God why he didn't save him. God replied, "I came to you three different times. First as a policeman, then as a fireman, and finally as a pilot. Each time you turned me away. I figured you didn't want my help!" As I recalled that story, I wondered if Maria's lawyer was God's way of helping us? I couldn't turn my back and walk away from that opportunity. It was imperative for us to seek out that lawyer and give her a chance to help us.

I called Maria to set up a meeting with her attorney. Maria told us that she thought we could have a baby in just a few days. I started to feel hopeful as we arranged a meeting for that evening at 7 p.m. Maria made me feel good about where the children were from. She reassured me that they were not black market babies. We had to wait ten hours for our meeting, but at least the lawyer worked on the weekends. Without the meeting, the weekend would have really dragged.

The weather was still overcast, rainy, damp, and miserable. Unfortunately, we didn't pack warm clothes, and we had been freezing since our arrival. If we were there long enough, it would warm up and we would be okay. I wondered what winters were like in Romania.

After breakfast, we sat in the hotel lobby and looked to see if the window had cracked any farther. We met Glenn and Janice there, watching the same crack, and ended up talking for several hours about each others experiences. It was refreshing to have friendships with other Americans. The hotel lobby was filled with American couples and became a common meeting place to share information and stories. Without those friendships we would have been even lonelier than we already were. It was hard to imagine, but the four of us just sat in the hotel lobby and laughed at the stories, and the things we had seen since arriving in Bucharest.

One of the most hilarious things we saw was a Romanian man who hung out at the InterContinental Hotel. We had no idea why he was in the lobby so much. We never saw him do any work. He could have been Benny Hill's twin brother and had the most hideous toupee in all of Europe. It not only was the wrong color and fit, but it was to his shoulders, where it blended in with his multicolored leisure suit.

Glenn told us about a local pediatrician who tested a sick child for an ear infection. The doctor cupped his hand and smacked the child's ear. If the child cried a little, than the ear was fine, but if the child really screamed, then there was an infection. We recalled hearing about a child who sat in a chair with a string of potatoes tied around her head. That treatment was thought to be a cure for a head ailment, or a headache. Julie, our friend living in Nicoresti, told us about a doctor's explanation for a woman who gave birth to a child with palsy. The doctor blamed the mother for the condition claiming that she drank alcohol during her pregnancy (and was drunk) thus causing the child to spend the rest of its life drunk. It was hard to believe that we found humor in those stories. Maybe it was a reflection of our frame of mind. Laughing helped our bodies to release endorphans, which modern medicine recognizes as a natural painkiller. We tried to laugh a lot, even over things that were not funny. Laughing just made us feel a whole lot better.

One thing that Pat couldn't laugh over was how the bar in the hotel overcharged him for our daily bottles of mineral water. Every day we would buy large bottles for 50 lei, and all of a sudden they started selling us small bottles for 75 lei. The cost of the water was not the issue, it was the principle that annoyed Pat.

Somehow we managed to kill the day, and before we knew it, it was time to meet with Maria's lawyer. The cold rain and overcast skies caused the night to come early. Armed with only an umbrella, we waved down a taxi cab and forced ourselves inside. We showed the driver the address as he sped away to this unknown destination. For some reason the driver refused to turn the windshield wipers on until he absolutely had to. With the fog building up on all of the windows, together with the intermittent use of the wipers, we couldn't tell where we were heading. Our only clue that we had arrived at our destination was when we no longer felt the car moving.

When we arrived, no one was home, and we thought we were being stood up or even worse, set up. I could handle being stood up, but not having thugs lurk behind the bushes in the darkness to rob us of our life savings. We thought a million different things as we stood there shivering, huddled under one tiny umbrella. We wondered why no one was there. We questioned if it was an honest business. Why did we have to meet at night? We tried to also think positive thoughts, like this may be the place where we could meet our child. It could be a wonderful place for us. We hung onto those warm thoughts, and made honest efforts to chase bad thoughts out of our minds.

We noticed that there was a children's hospital directly across the street. The place was busy with visitors coming and going, cheering up the patients inside. There were many children dressed in their pajamas and

robes wandering around outside in the damp
air. We wondered what was wrong with them.
We couldn't understand why they were out in
the damp night air if they were sick.

Finally after we had waited over an hour
in the pitch dark and freezing rain, a young
and handsome man slowly opened the heavy iron
gate and walked toward us through the lush
courtyard. In broken English he muttered,
"You are Maria's friend, you need help with
adoption?" After we both answered, "Yes"
simultaneously, he showed us in and introduced
us to his sisters. One was a lawyer; the
other was an interpreter. The three of them
scurried around the place as if they were
doing a million things at once. We saw how
the entire family worked together to match
children with adoptive parents. We realized
it was an honest business and we were glad we
decided to use their services. We sat alone
in a hallway for an hour before they told us
they knew of a beautiful newborn baby girl
that we could adopt.

My stomach was full of butterflies and I
told them that would be fantastic. I was
thinking that they couldn't be for real. I
wondered how we could be so lucky to get a
newborn baby. We had been in Romania for over
a week tormenting ourselves over how we were
going to find a baby. I only hoped that it
was real and that they would come through for
us. Part of me didn't want to get too
excited, but then Maria walked in with her
son, and he was a doll. That child was truly
a gift from heaven, and I prayed to God that
if we could get a child like Maria's, then I
would die a blessed person. Maria told me
that she was applying for her visa and heading
home in just a few days. I was glad for her
because I knew how miserable the adoption

process was, yet I wished she could stay a little bit longer with me. I told myself we would get together with our babies at home in America - Romania was no place to stay just to visit. Maria was lucky to be going home.

We were told we would get a phone call in three days to tell us the status of the orphaned baby girl. I thought I would fall apart if they didn't come through for us. As we were leaving we witnessed a French couple meeting their baby girl. It was such a wonderful feeling to experience. That couple took their tiny little bundle of joy and shared a taxi with us back to our hotel. I sat in the front seat with the driver, while Pat was crammed in the back with the couple and their new baby. While we tried to communicate in our foreign tongues, our nods, smiles, and scared apprehensions exchanged a million thoughts and words. With their wonderful French accents they told us that they were very scared, but the baby was so beautiful it was worth it all. It was a three-week-old girl. I wished it were me holding that baby. She was lucky to have that beautiful child. I only prayed that we too would be holding a baby soon.

Sunday May 26th: We were astonished over how many new Americans arrived daily in Bucharest despite the speculation that the adoptions were coming to a halt. We met a couple, Robin and Dave, who despite being in Romania only a few days, knew that there was a wonderful free breakfast buffet for all guests at the InterContinental Hotel. We couldn't believe that no one in the hotel bothered to tell us about that. We had been eating the damned rolls and tea for over a week and we were both sick of it. Robin showed me where the buffet was and I couldn't believe how fancy the restaurant was. For a moment, I thought I was in Paris. It was possible that after a week of doom and gloom, anything remotely nice would make me feel like I was in Paris. That was something to look forward to, a decent breakfast in a gorgeous dining room! Robin and Dave were trying to adopt two children and, because they had just arrived in Bucharest, they were in relatively good spirits. As time went on, we were to become each others support systems and help each other get through the adoption process.

The weather remained rainy and cold. Even though June was right around the corner, it felt like a late March afternoon. It allowed us to play the shut-in role and enjoy our last weekend alone as husband and wife. (We were being quite hopeful, but why not?) We had been sick for over a week with bad headaches and diarrhea and thought resting in our rooms might make us feel better. Actually the only thing that would make me feel better would be going home with a baby. We watched two news shows on the television: CNN and BBC. We were lucky to have those channels because no one else had them except the InterContinental Hotel.

Pat hooked up our walkman to the radio speaker in our room and we played cassettes that we had brought with us. For a brief moment it was like we were actually home on a rainy Sunday afternoon, playing music, sipping hot tea, and longing for a recent newspaper. The hotel did provide recent copies of Newsweek Magazine for all guests, which was a real treat to look forward to. We would share those magazines with our friends who were not staying in the hotel so they would be somewhat up to date on the current happenings in the world. It was amazing how we would share "news" as we heard it. Americans would get together and the first thing they would ask would be, "Anyone hear any recent news?" We hated the feeling that we were so isolated from home and the world we knew. We longed for it, and counted the days until we could be back and a part of it again.

We decided to make a calendar because I had not thought to bring one. I had no idea that we would be there so long with no end in sight, and counting the days would be crucial for our sanity. We had not realized that paper was in short supply, like everything else in Romania. We resorted to using the back of the card from Becky that I had found in my suitcase. It was appropriate: I looked at Becky's card so often, why not include a countdown calendar on it? We tried to project how long we would be there, and we both had the feeling that if we got out in a month, we would be lucky. That thought blew our minds as I didn't think I could last that long there. Furthermore, the hotel was very expensive, and we began to realize that we couldn't afford to stay there for four or five weeks. We also realized that Pat's vacation time from work was beginning to dwindle away.

Robin and Dave came by our room later in the afternoon and we spent the remainder of the day with them. It was great to have friends there. (Romania is a place where you really need to have friends in order to survive.) We told jokes and laughed the night away. At midnight, when they were leaving our room, I thought we were home seeing our guests out. Reality hit when they had to put their money belts back on to leave. We tucked our money belts under our pillows each night and hoped that our fairy godmother would come and turn it into a baby for us.

108

Monday May 27th: The weekend had not been nearly as bad as I thought it would be. We felt having friends made it to go by a little faster. We had two big things to look forward to on this day. The first was a wonderful breakfast buffet. The second was meeting Auriel's birth parents. The breakfast was nice and I enjoyed having a decent morning meal, but while I ate, I constantly thought about our meeting at the orphanage. Even the butterflies in my stomach were feeling sick. Lili was late picking us up. She was just as cold as ice to us because our lawyer told her she was finally being replaced per our request. She took it personally and held it against us. Lili was actually a very nice person, but we didn't feel that she was capable of accomplishing an adoption. In part because she had never done one before and was learning on our time with the doors about to close. I was not going to be happy unless we were assigned to an experienced and aggressive translator. That was what we were promised several months earlier when we first hired our attorney. We felt as if we had already wasted enough time. We needed to forge on and get our adoption moving along.

When we arrived at the orphanage, we were told that we were so late that we had missed the birth parents. I felt sick that we were so close and Lili had to pick us up late. We stood outside in the pouring rain in front of the orphanage wondering what to do next when a young Gypsy couple carrying a young child approached us. It was Auriel's birth parents returning to talk to us. Auriel's mother was twenty-three years old and had a beautiful face. She wore a yellow scarf over her long brown hair. She was dressed in a Hawaiian muumuu, size twenty, with a worn wool sweater.

She wore rags under her flip flops which left her feet cold and wet from the rain. She held a young child tightly in her arms and stayed close to her mate. He appeared to be older than she, and was a very slender and small-framed man. He wore many layers of torn and dirty clothes, but somehow I knew they were his best. He had dark and piercing brown eyes. In Romanian he said that we could adopt his son. I felt as if I might faint and I could feel myself going down, but somehow I managed to stay up. I took his face in my hands and said, "Thank you," at least a thousand times. My body was trembling and they each took our hands and kissed them. Lili told me to stop showing so much emotion because if they knew how badly we wanted their son, they could make a lot of demands on us. We were advised to act cool and to go to the car to talk with them.

The rain was cold but Mario had the taxi waiting. The couple sat inside the taxi and told Lili what they wanted from us while Pat and I stood outside in the downpour, waiting and wondering. We offered them food and clothes but they didn't want that. They demanded $1,200 converted into lei and a radio cassette. Pat and I were angry as that was not at all what we wanted to do. We asked them what they wanted the money for. When they wouldn't tell us, we told them we couldn't accept their offer. They were angry too and were about to leave when Pat and I thought that really it was a very small price to pay to get Auriel out of the orphanage and give him a good home back in America. We thought that we could tell Auriel someday that we gave the money because we knew that it would go to his biological brothers' and sisters' welfare. Somehow we justified it to ourselves and

110

figured that we had a lifetime to explain it to Auriel. We just wanted him out of that place. We were not the ones asking money for him. We didn't abandon him, they did. We were not the bad guys yet I somehow felt like we were. I looked into Pat's weepy eyes and said, "Pay them, let's get this over with so we can get Auriel home and show him what life is like outside of the orphanage walls."

Once we made the decision, there was a lot of work that needed to be done, and not very much time to complete it because the adoptions were going to stop in just a few days. The pressure was on us to make decisions fast, act fast, and get home fast. Without a second thought, I reached into my money belt with them looking on, and gave Mario $600 cash. I asked him to go to the black market and exchange it into lei for us as fast as he could. I looked at the birth father and told him, "You will get half now, and half after court." In the meantime we hired another set of taxis and raced around town in a whirl-wind trying to find a place where we could buy the radio cassette. We found a gigantic electronics store that was packed with hordes of people and tons of merchandise. I pointed to a cheap $50 cassette but Auriel's birth mother's face got real ugly as she screamed, "No" and pointed to a $300 fancy model. I was outraged that she didn't even have a pair of shoes on her feet yet she wanted a radio worth $300? The commotion started to cause others in the store to look at us with enormous curiosity. "What were these Americans doing here," they must have thought to themselves. "Why are they with Gypsies?" I had Lili translate every word but my facial expressions revealed the real story that I wouldn't pay over $100 and I wanted her

111

to pick out a model fast so we could get to the courts. The shopping spree took over an hour and was such a filthy experience for us. We were accused of paying for the cassette with counterfeit money. Pat was forced to reach down his pants to a hidden money belt for a crisper and cleaner $100 bill to pay for the radio.

By the time we reached the courthouse it was after noon. Mario arrived with the converted $600. We were about to hand it over when Auriel's father started making more demands. He wanted all of the money and the cassette player before signing the papers. I was infuriated, and disgusted beyond words about the entire episode. I felt all of my blood rush to my head and I knew my eyeballs were bulging out of my eye sockets. I felt the veins in my throat pulsating as my heart was rapidly beating out of control. I pointed my index finder approximately two inches from his crooked and ugly nose and in my meanest voice I told him that we had a deal, and if he couldn't honor it, then he could keep his son.

I asked myself, "How could I possibly work with this man to adopt Auriel when I no longer trusted him? What guarantee did we have that he would show up in court?" He could also have taken all of the money and stood up in court and announce that he changed his mind about the adoption. I asked him one last time if he would accept our original offer, and when he declined, I told him to go to hell, and to take his whole family with him. I told him the adoptions were over in just a few days and no one else could adopt Auriel because we had the only Commission paperwork. I told him he could have Auriel, that we no longer wanted him. We got into the taxi and I slammed the car door in their faces as Mario drove off leaving them empty-handed in the freezing cold rain. I looked at Pat with tear filled eyes praying that he wouldn't hate me for what I had just done. We both still wanted to adopt Auriel but we were not willing to give that man another dime. The entire day was like a bad dream, one we couldn't wake up from.

We were emotionally exhausted from that day of horror. We were chilled to the bone and soaking wet. The once-white leather moccasins I wore on my feet were so filthy they were unsalvageable. When we returned to our hotel room, I tried my best to wash them in the bathroom sink, but it didn't do much good. I tore my clothes off and threw them away. I took the longest and hottest shower that had ever been taken in that country. While the shower washed away the city's filth from my body, I wondered what it would take to get rid of the filth in my mind from that day. I put on my American blue jeans and my favorite sweat shirt. We were told not to wear them because we would stand out as rich Americans, but I no longer cared. I then called Robin to cry on her shoulder.

They had moved into a new apartment and invited us to see it. Getting out and being with friends was just what we needed after our miserable day. When we arrived at their apartment, there were about ten other Americans. They all listened to our shocking day, and then they told us their stories. We thought we had it bad, when in actuality, compared to some of the folks we just met, we really didn't have it so bad. That thought was incomprehensible. We were feeling so down on our luck. Apparently the other Americans felt the same way. I became so overwhelmed that I started to cry when I thought about how my sister exclaimed to me that her pregnancy was a miracle. I thought if I only got out of that country alive with a baby, that would be a miracle. While my sister was able to have five children, I only had the vision in my mind of Auriel and how I kissed his head when I told him that I would be back for him. Yet I knew that I never would be back for him. I would have to live with that on my conscience for the rest of my life.

We met Mark and Allison from Vermont who had the most beautiful baby in the world in their arms. As I held her, I prayed that somehow we could get over Auriel and find another baby. Yet it all seemed so hard to do. Mark and Allison were not without problems either. They had been in Romania for close to two months and the United States Government wouldn't issue their daughter a visa to get into America. I wondered why must we fight every step of the way. If we were not fighting with the Romanian officials, we had to fight with our own.

Allison was dressed so stylishly and looked absolutely adorable. I didn't think it was possible for anyone to look that good while pursuing an adoption in Romania. I showed Allison my passport photograph and told her, "That is what I look like when I am home." Then I realized how pathetic it was that my passport photo looked better than the real me. Irene, like so many other Americans, had been in Romania for several months alone without her husband, fighting to get their daughter out. One thing that we all had in common was that we were all fighting with a common goal and a common purpose. We were all experiencing similar difficulties, and we all had each other for support and friendship.

We returned to our hotel room hungry and fatigued. Pat made camper meals and we ate

114

them like zombies in the comfort of our beds. There was so much on our minds, and so much in our hearts, yet we felt too numb to convey our feelings to each other. We knew a good night's rest would do us both a world of good. We were just about to turn the lights out to go to sleep when the phone rang. It was Maria's lawyer. In mediocre English she said, "We have your baby girl, come get now."

# Chapter 8
# The Paper Chase

---

After hanging up the phone, Pat and I looked at each other in disbelief. We flew out of bed and ran around the room trying to get ready. Only in Romania could we lose a baby boy and find a baby girl in the same day. Merely a few short hours ago we were despondent over losing Auriel, and we were about to get a baby girl. Was it for real or were we dreaming? Talk about an emotional roller coaster! We were experiencing the ultimate anxiety attack, complete with confusion and elation. While "normal" couples get nine months to prepare and think about the arrival of their child, we got five minutes.

In our exhilarated state, we hailed a taxi and rushed to the lawyer's office to meet our daughter. I had no concept of time. Like other expectant parents, we paced the floor of the lawyer's lobby as if it were a hospital waiting room. I couldn't say how long it was before our daughter was carried into the office and handed to me. I didn't think to share the experience with Pat. I was completely absorbed in the moment, wanting to remember every detail. It was a feeling so passionate that I only recalled what our baby looked like and how I felt.

She was absolutely gorgeous. The red blanket that tightly bound her was drenched in urine, and only revealed her frail face. She was stiff as a board, and didn't make a peep.

I was concerned about her eyes as they were full of pus and appeared to be infected. There was a pediatrician at the office who offered to examine her for us for $10. We felt obligated to have the examination even though I didn't want it. As the doctor undressed the child, I couldn't believe how tiny that baby was. Her navel was still bloody and she had a severe case of diaper rash.

The lawyer told us that our baby was born on midnight and though the hospital nurses chose to put May 20th on her birth certificate, they named her Elena for having arrived on Saint Elena's day which was May 21st. The lawyer gave me a white knitted outfit to put the baby in. I knew it was not enough to keep her warm in the cool night air. I opened my coat and put her down my blouse for warmth. She wore three tiny caps on her head, so at least her head would be warm.

We gave the taxi driver a gift of soaps and cigarettes to wait for us. Thankfully the cab was warm, exactly what we needed. A million thoughts raced though our minds as we rode back to the hotel that evening. With the baby crying and opening her tiny and sore eyes to look at me, I knew that it was going to be all up to me. I had to keep her safe, warm, and well, and somehow get her home. I couldn't imagine my sister having to ride home in the dead of the night, in some foreign country, in a taxi where the driver couldn't speak a word of English, with a newborn baby in her arms. I was not going back to the comfort of my home, but to a strange hotel with a road of red tape waiting in front of me. We had a million things that needed to be done in order to get our child home. She wouldn't be ours until we were home, safe in

America. She could have AIDS. It could all backfire on us – and I had thought things would be better once we had a baby in our arms. Well actually, things were a lot better having a baby in our arms. I knew deep down inside there was a good chance that this child would be our daughter. All I had to do was take each step, no matter how big, one at a time, and keep her alive. I felt as if I could do that. With God's help, and with Pat's, we had a good chance at keeping the baby.

As I walked into the hotel with this tiny baby in my arms I was filled with enormous feelings of happiness and warmth. We accepted that there was always going to be the possibility that something could go wrong with the adoption, or the lawyers could demand more money. I knew that things could quickly go down hill on us and we could lose her just as fast as we had found her. Yet there was a feeling inside of me that I hung onto with all of my power which enabled me to be glad to hold that child and be proud to "almost" be a parent. I tried to walk fast through the hotel lobby so I wouldn't be noticed. I couldn't hide the smile that for so long was a stranger to my face. I wanted the adoption to work. We were definitely getting closer to accomplishing our goal.

As we rode in the elevator up six flights, I told Pat that we shouldn't get attached to that adorable child in the event that we must give her back. As awful as it seemed, we thought that we could give her better care than a foster home in Romania. We therefore considered ourselves to be only temporary foster parents. We wanted to call her "baby" until we reached America. However, as soon as we reached our room, the first thing we did

118

was to baptize her, naming her Juliana, which means youthful one.

We gave her a bath in the sink, which she hated, and then I rubbed antibiotic cream all over her body. We put her in one of the warm outfits that I had brought from home. Pat nervously read and reread the directions on how to mix the formula. I gave her a warm bottle with extra fortified vitamins, and laid her down to sleep in a bed made from a dresser drawer. When she finally went to sleep, I stood over her, watching her, and prayed to God that we could keep her. I was trying not to bond with her, but she was so adorable it was hard not to. When she cried I would pick her up and sing, "God Bless America" and "America the Beautiful." I couldn't remember any lullabies and didn't know any other songs to sing her. Occasionally I would switch to religious songs, but they made me cry. I had to stick to patriotic songs which gave me inner strength, and something magnificent to look forward to - going home.

Tuesday May 28th: It was strange for us to walk into a fancy restaurant for our breakfast with a baby. Only one day earlier we didn't have a baby, and now we did. Magic in Romania. This eight-day-old infant took it all in as if it were normal. I doubt we would have taken an eight-day-old infant out to breakfast if we were in America. Only in Romania could you find newborns going out to dinner in restaurants with their parents. Other Americans would walk up and ask, "Oh you have such a beautiful baby, how wonderful! When did you get her?" It was not at all like a question to be asked back home.

The damp weather forced us to expose our baby to the elements as we made our way to the hospital for her blood tests. We hired a taxi and headed to the Policlinica Titan, which was one of the two reliable facilities in all of Bucharest equipped to perform AIDS and hepatitis tests. We found the hospital to be nearly as damp and depressing as every other Romanian building we had encountered. Many of the windows were cracked, which allowed the rain and wind to whip throughout its hallways, exposing everyone inside, including the patients. I knew I was freezing and I was not sick. I couldn't imagine being sick in Romania and requiring hospitalization. The halls were very dark, since many of the burned out light bulbs had never been replaced. The huge cracks in the floors and walls made you wonder if there had been a recent earthquake. There was filth everywhere. Everyone wore heavy coats inside the hospital in an attempt to keep warm. Even the doctors and nurses wore coats over their uniforms.

We arrived at 9 a.m. and waited until noon for a lab attendant to see us, only to find out that we were in the wrong department. A kind Romanian, who spoke some English, told us that we were indeed in the wrong place and pointed to where we needed to be. We ran down three flights of stairs and quickly found the correct laboratory. I tried to explain to the doctor that we had been waiting for several hours in the wrong department and asked her to kindly draw our baby's blood for AIDS and hepatitis testing. The beautiful woman looked at her watch and said, "I am so sorry, it is now a few minutes after noon and we don't draw blood after noon." I began to cry and I pleaded with her to do us a favor. We explained that we were trying to complete the adoption before the government closed the doors to all of the adoptions in a matter of a few days. I remembered the gift I brought with me and I set it on her desk. When she saw the tears in our eyes, and the gift, she changed her mind and said she would make an exception because we looked like nice people. I am certain it was the satin bag filled with cosmetics and candy that helped persuade her to perform the tests for us. The doctor told Pat to pay for the test and left me to assist in drawing the baby's blood.

I brought all of my own syringes, needles, and test tubes, and was prepared to draw the blood myself but the doctor was very confident. For some unknown reason, I trusted that she would do it right. With the baby laying across my legs, the nurse inserted a needle into her vein. The blood gushed out while the doctor caught it in the test tube. There was blood everywhere, and I found it hard to believe that, though I had brought plastic gloves, the doctor chose not to use them. When the test tube was half full, she removed the needle and the procedure was over. That gruesome, archaic procedure was what I waited three hours for. I trembled during the entire episode, praying to God that those tests would be negative.

Meanwhile, Pat was held up at the cashier's office, leaving me to wait for over an hour with the doctor. During that time I had a nice conversation with the doctor and we began to understand each others' circumstances. She wanted to leave her homeland and live in America with her brother who worked as a dentist in Rochester, New York. I couldn't help but believe her when she told me how difficult it was for her to live in her country. I told her that I worked in a laboratory in America in a city close to Rochester where her brother lived. My words were genuine when I told her that if she ever

121

comes to America to visit her brother, she should also plan to visit me. She came to respect me for also having laboratory experience and proudly gave me a few demonstrations on how she performs certain studies using chemicals that were probably lethal. When Pat finally finished the paper work, we needed to provide the patient's name for the blood test. Even though we said we were not going to give the baby a name, it was impossible not to. That was the first time we officially used her name, Juliana Elena Canale.

We arrived back at the hotel at 4 p.m. I kissed Juliana on the head and told her how proud I was of her for holding up so well under such terrible conditions. I had to remind myself not to kiss our child because I didn't want to get attached to her. She had been with us less than 24 hours and already she had become a part of us.

Wednesday May 29th: We sat with several Canadian couples at breakfast who gave us a lot of good advice. We were clearly rookies and that was just what we needed having been parents for only one day. Pat and I had no nurses or relatives to help us, but we all had each other. We discovered that the hotel provided free cribs, so we immediately ordered one for Juliana. It felt wonderful to lay our baby in a crib, where she belonged. I slid the drawer back in the dresser where it was meant to be.

The rain began to taper off and even though it was still cold and overcast, we went out to see if we could buy some warmer baby clothes. We found a tiny shop down the street from the hotel. The only thing we could find was a pink sweater for 400 lei or $2.42. Juliana was so small she couldn't fit into the three outfits that I had for her. We meandered down a cobblestone street close to the United States Embassy, and came across a meat market. Inside there were whole pigs hanging from the ceiling. We bought some Romanian chocolates and wafer cookies that had been imported from Israel. Food from the Middle East tasted great and was well worth buying regardless of the price. We paid an unbelievable $7.00 for one quart of orange juice imported from Israel.

We saw another store called Magazin, which was filled with people. We made our way through the crowd to see what all of the commotion was about. The store was completely empty except for a few items such as toothpaste and soap that were scattered about on a small shelf. People just looked at those items but apparently were unable to afford them. I was perplexed over the shopping methodologies. I couldn't understand how stores could be empty except for a few little things that cost next to nothing and still no one could afford to buy them. I did find one upscale clothing and department store that had some merchandise in it. However, people were not allowed to touch the goods. I couldn't comprehend why anyone would buy something that they couldn't even touch. I tried to touch something, but the big velvet ropes prevented me from getting too close to the counters. There were a few mannequins in the window that were dressed in outfits that must have been fifty years old. The mannequins had blank and empty stares in their lifeless bodies, much like those we saw every day in the Romanian people while walking the streets in Bucharest.

Many of the adopting couples shopped at a store named Jupiter's. It was located in a principle shopping district on Victoria

Street, Bucharest's version of 5th Avenue. The store had imported milk from Iran one day, a real treat. I wanted to buy a liter bottle at a bargain price of $2.00 but I only had Romanian currency with me and the store would accept only American dollars. No one really appreciated that unwritten ripoff policy that many Romanian business dictated to its foreign shoppers. We heard that many goods, such as electronics, could only be bought with hard currency. It didn't matter who was making the purchase, a Romanian or a foreigner. The Yankee dollar was quite a valuable and desirable commodity in Romania.

I observed an American who purchased her goods with U.S. dollars. She became angry when the store's clerk told her to select thirty cents worth of candy, because they chose not to give back her due change of thirty cents. To the adopting community, Jupiters was known for its hideous dresses in the store's window with K-Mart price tags dangling from the sleeve. The store also carried Pedos, which were the Romanian equivalent to Pampers. Adopting couples knew that Jupiters was one of the few places that carried disposable diapers. No matter when you went there, chances were that you would run into a desperate adopting parent whose supply of diapers had run dry!

We joined Dave and Robin at the InterContinental Hotel for one of our favorite Romanian dishes, goulash soup. We wondered what type of meat was used in the preparation of that soup. With every spoonful, we hesitated slightly, recalling how people would tease us that rat meat was abundant, and sometimes used in Romanian cooking. Nevertheless, we still enjoyed the soup along with a plentiful supply of rolls and mineral water.

Afterward, we went back to their apartment to visit with the group of Americans that socialized there. It was an especially sad day for Mark and Allison who were officially denied their daughter's visa into America. It was not only sad for them, but it rudely awakened us to the fact that we too could have our visas denied. It was incomprehensible to think that we could cut through all of the red tape, jump through every hoop placed in front of us, and when it came time to get our visas to leave, the United States Government said, "No." Why, then, did the government allow us to start the adoption process, only to tell us that we had legally adopted a child that couldn't come home with us? Nothing in Romania made sense to me.

When we returned to our hotel room, we ate yet another camper meal for dinner. Usually it reminded us of home and it picked up our spirits, but for some reason we were depressed and nothing seemed to help. We longed to be back home in the normal routines we left behind. We missed our families and Sparkey. We felt sickened from the adoption process and wished it would be over soon. Pat's phone call to his parents seemed to lift his spirits a little bit. I felt worse after I talked to my mom and dad. I broke down crying to them about how difficult it was living there and working on the adoption. We told our families that we had a baby girl. We had to remind them that she wouldn't be ours until after many obstacles were overcome. We prayed that her blood tests for hepatitis and AIDS would be normal. We hoped we would obtain the formal adoption decree and get her a visa. We had so much to do before we could call her "ours." Actually, I felt that this child

would be mine for only a short time. Time
enough for me to take care of her and watch
her grow up before my very eyes. As crazy as
it seemed, I wanted her to stay that sweet and
innocent forever, and never grow up. Juliana
was actually more beautiful than any baby I
ever dreamed of having. Her face was pure and
heaven-like. She was our Romanian angel.

Mark and Allison had given me some
medicine for Juliana's eye infection. I
didn't even know what it was, but it worked.
Her diaper rash was almost healed too. So
often, I would talk to God and beg him to give
me a beautiful baby, but I never once thought
I would get one so perfect. I was afraid that
something would go wrong with the adoption,
and I dreaded the thought of giving her back.
It seemed cruel to have to hand her back to a
system that had no plans for her growth and
development. Pat and I agreed that if the
adoption didn't work out with Juliana, we were
not going to try anymore. We would cut our
losses and go home without a baby. We would
have given it a good fight and tried our very
best. We had decided to accept whatever God
had in store for us. We could only hope that
it included Juliana.

Thursday May 30th: We woke up to a
frantic phone call from Robin and Dave. They
were on their way to get their baby and needed
more Kent cigarettes. My heart went out to
them, as I knew how strenuous it was for them.
Thoughts of meeting Auriel were still too
fresh in my mind, and I only prayed that their
meeting went smoother than ours. As the sun
began to rise, we embraced each other and they
departed with the cigarettes and our warm
wishes. My heart was in my throat as we
watched them leave, hoping they would be
successful.

We quickly got ready to return to the hospital where Juliana had had her blood tests. We needed the test results before our lawyer could set the court date. In our hearts we felt the test results would be negative, yet we knew there was a possibility that Juliana could have AIDS or hepatitis like thousands of other Romanian children. The apprehension we felt was escalating as the taxi approached the hospital. We held each other's hands as we walked in silence down the cold hospital corridor. Our hearts were beating out of control when we arrived at the laboratory door. When we approached the doctors office we were petrified to walk inside until we saw a big smile on the doctor's face when she recognized us and knew why we were there. Once again, our prayers were answered when she told us that Juliana's test results were normal. Because the laboratory lacked modern equipment, Pat and I knew that we would have to have Juliana retested once we were home. For the time being, we had to accept that she was fine, and be content with being one step closer to bringing her home.

When we returned to our hotel room, Maria called to say her visa was approved and she was going home. With the United States Embassy turning so many Americans down, it was good to hear that someone was approved. Knowing that we used the same lawyer, maybe we would also be successful getting a visa. I was immediately overwhelmed with sadness knowing Maria was leaving. I was glad for her, but sad for me. It had been reassuring knowing she was just a short distance away. Her phone calls and support would be missed. It was great to talk to someone I knew from home. She offered to give me $200 and all of her left-over food since Pat and I were running low on food and didn't know how much longer we would be there. It was pouring rain, so I couldn't meet Maria at the Embassy to say good-bye, but Pat met her there and wished her well.

I was going to have Maria deliver a letter to mom and dad for me, but I couldn't find the right words to write. I held a pen in my hand for over an hour. Every time I would begin to write something, I would start crying. My choice of words reflected my feelings and pitiful state of mind. I didn't want my parents to be depressed over the letter and to worry any more than they already were. I finally told Maria that I ran out of time and didn't write my parents a letter. I did ask her to call them and tell them that we were all right. We asked Maria not to relay the realities that were continuously facing us and to lie to my folks if she had to about Romania so they didn't worry. I knew what I asked of Maria was wrong, but at that time, I was not thinking clearly. Maria left a letter she had written to me before she departed. I must have read it a million times. She was so lucky to be going home. I started dreaming about going home too.

The food Maria gave us couldn't have come at a better time. We were filled with excitement as we savored the goodies, as if we were enthusiastic children looking through a basket the Easter Bunny had just left us. We also found a deck of cards tucked neatly in the care package which helped pass the time away and granted us many hours of fun playing "Go Fish" and "Old Maid."

Friday May 31st: After breakfast we walked around the city and stumbled upon a bakery where we ordered one kilogram of eclairs. They cost $1.20 for a mountain of luscious confections. We visited Robin and Dave who had an eleven-month-old boy, Jason. They were looking for an infant sister for their adorable son. The entire day was spent visiting friends and trying to relax and not think about going home. We had nothing to do but kill time and wait for our court date. We visited Candy and her fifteen-month-old daughter, Sarah, whose visa had been denied. They were applying for Humanitarian Parole and hoped to make it home by that route. By the end of the day we were exhausted from all of the visiting we had done and headed back to our room.

We received a call from Roy, a friend from Syracuse who had recently adopted a baby from Romania. He called to reassure us that we would be okay and to remind us not to get discouraged. Those words seemed more valid coming from someone who knew exactly what we were up against. Because Roy had recently walked the path we faced, we heeded his advice, and appreciated his words of wisdom.

Saturday June 1st: Our frantic month of May had ended. It was rumored that all of the adoptions were suspended until further notice. The government would try to regulate and organize their adoption laws during the time the doors were closed. We placed an urgent phone call to our Romanian attorney to be sure that we were not affected by the suspension. She reassured us that as long as we had a court date filed, we would be okay. We did have a court date filed but didn't know exactly when it would be. Needless to say, that made us very nervous. Everything in Romania made us nervous - we should have been used to it.

We visited a very depressed Mark and

129

Allison, who had decided to leave Romania without their daughter. They had been in Romania for six weeks and were extremely stressed out from their draining adoption ordeal. Because they had no idea when their baby's visa would be approved, they chose to wait at home instead of waiting in Romania. Without Pat and I even discussing it, we agreed to offer to bring their baby home for them, saving them from making another long and expensive flight back. We were hoping to be leaving soon too, and the timing couldn't be better.

They told us that we could move into their apartment and encouraged us to look at it. The place was awful but the price was right. It was close to the Embassy and location was worth everything in Bucharest. The apartment was located in the rear lower section of the complex making it seem as if we had to walk through a rat maze to find it. The halls were pitch dark and the floors echoed our clumsy footsteps as we walked through the damp corridors. Their apartment consisted of one small room with two mattresses on the floor. The walls were painted with glitter. There was a large window that had external wooden blinds which obliterated the sunlight. With great difficulty, the blinds could be opened and some of the sunlight reflected off the glitter painted on the walls. There was a very tiny kitchen that housed a small gas stove and sink along with one cupboard.

The small bathroom was so filthy, I was not sure that I could use it. The bathroom floor was black, cold, and slippery. There was a floor drain next to the toilet and I expected to see a monster crawl out of it. The tub was surrounded by yellow tile that had years of mildew growing on it. The bathroom sink was broken and the water ran constantly. We never would have thought that we would come to hate the bathroom and the sound of water constantly gurgling in the drain. The apartment cost $90 per week. We recognized how essential it was to start saving our money. We wondered how bad it could be if Mark and Allison had lived there. Besides, we thought we would be leaving Romania soon. We met the landlord and told him that we couldn't pay American dollars for the room. Instead our offer was to give him 17,000 lei which gave him a bonus of $13 for taking some of our lei off of our hands. We still had a lot of Romanian currency left over from the transaction made with Auriel's birth parents and we needed to get rid of it. Slowly but surely we exchanged it with other Americans who needed lei but we still had so much of it that we had to carry it around in a satchel. We were known as "The Bank of Canale" to the other adopting couples.

We met Robin and Dave in the alley by their apartment and bought pizzas for lunch. They were small individual pizzas which cost only 37 lei (22c total or 5c per person for lunch.) Pizza Hut does make a better pizza, but prices here were hard to beat. It was difficult to complain about a personal pan pizza if it only cost a nickel.

Eventually several couples gathered in our room and Mark and Allison were among them. It was a somber feeling knowing that they were leaving without their baby. We were glad that we were able to help them by bringing their daughter home for them. They were half glad to be leaving, and half sad to leave their baby.

We were celebrating our last night at the InterContinental Hotel. We were checking out

in the morning and were apprehensive about
moving into the apartment. We had become
accustomed to the Romanian style of luxury at
the hotel, and we knew that the dirty,
pathetic apartment that we were moving into
would make the hotel room seem like a palace.
After all, I enjoyed the cable television and
the privilege of a telephone with an overseas
operator. We asked Mark to call my parents
from Vermont and give them our new phone
number in the apartment so they would know
where we were. While the hotel had heat or
air-conditioning, the apartment was very cold
and damp. The hotel had hot showers, while
the apartment at times had no water at all.
Cold water was a luxury for the apartment. We
knew we didn't have the money to live in
luxury forever, and we had to start saving
somewhere, as our trip had cost us dearly. We
thought it was a small sacrifice to make.

That night we went out for an early dinner
with Dave and Robin at a restaurant called
Casa Capcha. It was a short walk from their
apartment down Victoria Street. As we paraded
down the street we saw a newly married bride
leaving a photography studio. She looked
beautiful and so happy in her traditional
white lace gown. Encircling her was a band of
musicians who wore folk costumes while they
played their flutes. The gallant tune they
were playing was catching as we continued to
hum it walking past them on our way to the
restaurant. The dining room was casual and we
were their only patrons. Back home this might
signal a restaurant with lousy food. It was
definitely not the case at that establishment.
I had the most scrumptious beef stroganoff,
and chocolate cake. Our dinner cost only
$2.72 for two wonderful meals. We left the
restaurant after 9 p.m. and were scared

walking back to the hotel in the dark. We knew it was unsafe for us to be out that late, but we got carried away having fun.

Earlier in the day we heard rumors that several Irish couples had their babies stolen by secret police for not carrying the adoption papers. We didn't have one single paper for Juliana, and I would die if a secret policeman stole her from me. We began to realize how important it was to keep a low profile until we got Juliana's documents. It certainly did put additional pressure on us to always watch over our shoulders to make sure no one would steal her from us. It was never a concern to us prior to hearing the rumors. Things changed fast in Romania, and we had to change with them in order to survive.

Before going to sleep, we sat on the beds that we once made fun of for having such a thin and sunken mattress. We gave a moment's thanks for having stayed in the hotel for as long as we had. Juliana would soon have to sleep in a basket that Candy gave us instead of her nice crib. Life in the apartment would teach us a little bit about what life in Romania would be like. I thought it would do us good to "rough it" a little more. We had been quite spoiled living in the hotel.

I knew we would really miss the elegant breakfast buffets in the fancy French-style restaurant. In the apartment we would have to go to the bakery each day or just make do with what we had. For some reason, I was having a lot of trouble letting go of the hotel. I was sure it was because I had become accustomed to the western style of living. The Inter-Continental wouldn't have received a five star rating from AAA. It was far from luxury. Once we realized what normal Romanian living standards were, we had more than most in the hotel, but it was still far from American luxury. I started to realize that we were going to be living in conditions that I was not accustomed to.

To maintain my sanity, I continually reminded myself that we were saving close to $3,000 by checking out of the hotel. I had a newborn infant in a third world country. I just wanted to go home to the comfort of my own home. I wanted my jacuzzi, and my microwave oven. I wanted fresh brewed hot coffee in the morning with a bagel and gobs of cream cheese smothered all over it. I wanted to reach into my refrigerator and have a diet Coke with ice whenever I wanted one. I wanted a big thick juicy steak cooked on the grill with corn on the cob with tons of butter drizzling off it. I wanted a big tall glass of whole milk with oreo cookies before I hopped into my queen-size four poster bed, made with crisp clean sheets. The cold reality was that I was experiencing a bad case of homesick blues and leaving the hotel would only amplify it. I really just wanted to go home. I didn't want to go from bad to worse. However, recognizing that the move would be financially worthwhile, we packed our bags and got ready to check out in the morning. I knew I was capable of being a strong person. I dug deep into my pockets looking for some extra strength to get me through the days that were ahead of me. I had to stand up tall, dust myself off, and force myself to keep going.

# Chapter 9
# Life in the Apartment

---

June second was our last free breakfast in the hotel. It was convenient to be served a decent meal in elegance each morning. In the apartment we didn't know where our breakfasts would come from. With that thought in mind, I took a second stroll down the buffet line and filled my pockets with bruised apples and pastries. My eyes were fixed on the platter of tomatoes, cucumbers, and cheese. I didn't even enjoy eating them for breakfast, yet I thought about taking some for later anyway.

Before checking out, Pat had already estimated what the room bill would be, including our many phone calls to the states. When we received the bill we discovered that they overcharged us $55 per night. We knew our bill was going to be high considering we had been staying for several weeks but it was outrageous. Apparently the hotel raised its rates due to a world trade convention that had been going on in Bucharest. Pat really blew his top, but it only made matters worse. The bellboy then confiscated our luggage after the maid accused us of stealing towels. We were furious, and felt as if we were hostages in a country without any rights.

We soon learned that we could be subjected to such inconveniences as long as we were guests in Romania. Pat fought a useless battle with the management staff for over an hour. I was not able to stay with him during the confrontation because I had to meet with the landlord. I ran out of things to talk about with the landlord while waiting for Pat to arrive with the money to pay the rent. Eventually Pat was able to get the bellboy off his back about the towels. Fearing that he would be arrested, Pat ended up paying the entire inflated hotel bill. He vowed that the InterContinental Hotel had not heard the last of it and that we would never stay in one of their hotels again! Times like that we had to shrug our shoulders and try to laugh it off saying things like, "Only in Romania could something like this happen." We couldn't imagine something like that going on at a Holiday Inn.

The landlord of the apartment graciously accepted our offer of $103 for one week's stay in his dingy studio apartment. We figured he probably paid the equivalent of $100 for an entire year to live in that apartment and was making a bundle of money off the Americans to whom he rented it. Some of the Romanians were catching on to capitalism. He forgot to bring us a set of clean sheets and towels, and thought nothing of making us wait a day or two for clean ones. We knew Mark and Allison had been using the room's only sheets and towels for over three weeks, and we were not going to use them. I told the landlord to buy new linens with the money we just gave him, allowing him the entire day to provide us with clean sheets and towels. By the evening we did have new muslin sheets and polyester towels in our room.

The landlord bought the radio cassette that we had bought to give to Auriel's birth parents. Even though we paid $95 for it, we gave it to him for $65. As an extra bonus, we threw in a few Vanilla Ice tapes that Robin and Dave had given us. American music was hot in Romania, and even though we didn't particularly care to listen to Vanilla Ice, cassette tapes of any rock and roll band could quickly turn a "no" into a "yes" in any given situation. Most important of all, music, this universal language, could buy you food, when no food existed. The word "no" in Romania does not mean no if you have the right "gift." It was incredible how quickly I learned to fight for things when I wouldn't take no for an answer. The right "gift" got us the blood test at the hospital when we were just a few minutes late. We found that some of the Romanians really liked to hear Americans cry for things. Reluctantly, we learned their tricks and played their games, to get what we wanted.

Though our morning started off poorly, we didn't let it ruin the rest of our day. I was glad to be out of the hotel, no longer feeling paranoid wondering if our room was bugged. Being able to unload the radio cassette really made our day. Considering the fact that I was going to throw it off the top of the hotel and watch it smash on the ground below, I was happy to have the $65 for it. The best part about that day was that the weather finally cleared. The sun and warmth helped to pick up our spirits. We were grateful for the blue skies which permitted us to make plans to go to the Museum Village in Bucharest. It reminded us of an Indian village or colonial village that we would have in America. For a moment, I thought I was back in America, touring in some part of the country I had never seen before. The village was a replica of the outer provences within Romania, and depicted how the Romanians used to live many years ago. We thoroughly enjoyed walking

137

throughout the park, outside in the sunshine, away from the restlessness of the city.

We walked through a lush garden on our way back to the city where we knew it would be easier to locate a taxi. It was too far for us to walk the entire way back to the apartment, especially carrying Juliana who was getting heavier to carry. Finding taxis was actually quite easy because drivers could spot Americans a mile away. They knew that chauffeuring Americans yielded a higher profit. The ride didn't cost them any more, but Romanians knew that most Americans had money and they too wanted a piece of the American pie. A typical ride for a Romanian could cost only 35 lei, but the same ride would cost an American 100 lei. We started to pay the taxi drivers with the many leftover gifts we had brought with us. We found the drivers especially liked the fancy soaps and cosmetics. Whenever we gave gifts for our ride, the driver never failed to get out and open the doors for us. During the first week in Romania when we paid for taxi rides in lei, the car would barely come to a stop before we got out.

One cab driver was very friendly and told us that a gift meant far more to his family than 100 lei. After all, what value did money have in a society where there were few goods available? The drivers, who were always men, gave the gifts to their mothers or wives, or saved them for a special occasion. The special occasion could be a trip to the doctors office where a gift was almost always required for them to get an appointment. We were told that they came in handy when a family member was sick and medicine was needed. Gifts would always buy medicine. It was hard to imagine living like that but the

Romanians we met were accustomed to it. We would never forget one taxi cab that came with air-conditioning. It was the hottest ride of our lives. At the red light, the driver, who insisted on keeping the windows up, had to open his door to let some cool air inside. When we finally reached our destination, Pat's shirt was soaked with perspiration. Perhaps the driver wanted to keep the wind off Juliana.

Upon returning to our apartment in the early afternoon, we discovered that my wallet was missing from my purse. I had about $50 in it, but it also contained my Mastercard and a few other things that were important to me. I began to cry uncontrollably. For me, it was my way of releasing the frustration I felt over losing my wallet. The noise of my crying echoed off the four walls in that tiny apartment which drove Pat wild. I never saw him go mad until that moment. He tore the apartment apart looking for it. I knew all along that we just moved in and there was no way I would have ever taken my wallet out of my purse. Pat wouldn't accept that. In a fit of rage, he insisted we return to the hotel where we were told to never step foot in again. Pat confronted the manager who remembered him from the morning. I knew we were burned out from our exhausting trip, and the issue of the wallet was had taken an unnecessary toll on us both. Pat once again persuaded a bellboy to allow us to look through our old room. Low and behold, Pat found the wallet hidden under the mattress with all of our credit cards and cash, just where he left it! He was so happy he could have kissed the bellboy, but graciously tipped him as he ran out of the room. Later we talked about how we had overreacted to that incident. We promised each other to try to keep one another levelheaded if something like that should happen again.

In the hotel lobby we met and became friends with Steve and Carol. Much to our surprise they had hired the same U.S. law firm to help them with their adoption. Steve and Carol found the attorneys had misrepresented them also by not providing the services they paid for. This couple didn't want to go home without a child, so they did much of the adoption process on their own. It took them two months to adopt a sibling pair of toddlers. Living in Romania had taken an enormous emotional toll on them both. It was apparent when their eyes filled with tears as we spoke fondly of the lifestyles we had left behind us.

We found a nice clothing store nestled in among other rundown shops with near empty shelves. We were able to buy Juliana several sweater outfits for a few dollars. The smallest size that I bought would probably fit her at Christmas. She was so tiny, that I couldn't find anything that would fit her. As we walked back to the apartment, we reflected on our day which had had many peaks and valleys. One minute we were very angry, the next we were remarkably happy. Tense moments were soon followed by peaceful periods. Then our moods turned to frustration which gradually migrated to placid, calm feelings. All of these feelings were extremes to our emotional spectrum. Nevertheless, we were ending the day on a good note.

When the day was over, we knew it was time to settle into the tiny room we would call home for a brief period in our lives. As we began to spread the scratchy sheets on the mattress, the room's only light bulb blew out.

We sat in the dark and thought about how Mark and Allison were doing. We wondered if they had made it home yet, and how they had managed to live in the tiny, dirty apartment before us. We also wondered how the landlord managed to live there when he was not renting it out. I thought about how horrifying it must have been to live there while the revolution was going on just outside. We were cold and it was June – how cold must it get in January? Romania was a scary place for us to visit. I could have thought all night, considering what it would be like living in Romania permanently, but I knew that deep down I really didn't care to know how bad it could actually get. I only wanted to go home.

The room was pitch dark and our only source of light was one small flashlight and a candle. Pat fumbled around in the dark, lighting the candle every time Juliana would get us up for a bottle during the night. Suddenly I was wishing we were back in the hotel. As I laid back down and tried to relax enough to fall asleep, I could feel something crawling on me and biting me. I danced around the tiny room in the dark, whirling my flashlight uncontrollably in every single direction trying to spot something. I couldn't see any bugs crawling around so reluctantly I laid back down and cried myself to sleep. I was sure that something like that wouldn't have happened in the hotel.

Monday June 3rd: We woke up to sunshine again for the second day in a row. The sun really lit up the apartment. It was nice after being helpless in the dark all night. The bright rays allowed us to see that the apartment had never been cleaned. There was more dirt on the floor than on our garage floor back home. Under the Ceausescu regime

141

vacuum cleaners had been outlawed, so that precious energy could be preserved. This luxury machine had only been found in the homes of the wealthy or Communist leaders.

It was essential for me to dwell on the positives there, and sunshine again was something to be grateful for. In addition, we had not had diarrhea for two consecutive days. We felt doubly lucky! I even found a strawberry poptart in our suitcase and Pat and I jumped up and down with excitement as if we had won the million dollar lottery. It was only a poptart, but it tasted ten times better than any poptart ever tasted at home. Our morning was certainly off to a great start.

We placed a call to our lawyer in an attempt to pin her down on a court date. We were feeling very confident and felt as if we had the courage to get a little more aggressive with finishing up the adoption. Our attorney was not in but the housekeeper told us that our lawyer had arranged our court date for us. We were elated. Our attorney made it easy for us, for a price of course, but it was worth it to save our mental health.

After we told Robin and Dave our good news, they invited us over to celebrate. We were not ready for a celebration yet. They did however buy some of our lei from us. We were down to only $200 from the $600 we had converted for Auriel's birth parents. When we realized that we still had $200 in lei, we thought we should go out shopping and spend it on Juliana. We wanted to buy her something to teach her about the country of her birth. I was able to buy her a few authentic outfits that I saw in the window of a small shop. We found it difficult to buy something that was in the window. For some reason, shopkeepers didn't like to ruin their window displays.

Often we noticed that items in the displays were not available inside the store. For a price, I was able to buy Juliana a few adorable children's-sized outfits from a window display. We bought her dolls, flutes, records, books, tapestries and blankets. We put a lot of effort into selecting things that we hoped she would like, taking into consideration that there was not a lot of things to buy, since many stores were empty. We really did have a lot of fun shopping and the best part was that we didn't spend over $25. In America the things we bought would have cost at least $500.

We thought about getting passport photos taken of Juliana. If things started to progress quickly, we wanted to be ready so that we could leave the country on a moment's notice. We hired an extremely nice taxi driver to help us find a photography studio. He knew of a shop called "Baby Photo" near the InterContinental Hotel. They agreed to provide overnight service at a reasonable rate of $3. The studio, like most places in Romania, was small and dimly lit. From where I sat, I could see old and tattered stuffed animals piled in the corner. I held Juliana while the photographer snapped several angles of her head. I thought about how couples back home have professional nursery photographs taken of their newborn infants before they leave the hospitals where they were born. I wished that option was available for me, but because it was not, the "Baby Photo" session was the best I could offer my baby. We were hoping that we would be able to find the photography studio again to pick up the pictures. Streets and buildings in Bucharest all looked alike, and it was easy to get lost.

We went for a walk before dinner and found

a bottle of orange Fago pop for sale at a
street side stand for 225 lei, which was
expensive for Romania, $1.36 for one liter.
It was hot outside and I was dying of thirst.
Pat and I opened it up and drank the entire
thing on the sidewalk. I later wished that I
had bought more then, because though we looked
for it everywhere we went, we never found it
again. We saved the plastic bottle just like
a typical Romanian would. That way we could
make a bottle of Tang and carry it with us.
We made macaroni and cheese with a can of tuna
in it for dinner, and it was fantastic. At
home we might turn our noses up to a dinner
like that but Pat and I devoured a meal large
enough to serve four people. We were
especially hungry.

I was feeling exceptionally tired, achey,
and feverish, but didn't attribute it to
anything. I noticed that I had a bad bug bite
on my upper leg. I wondered if it was from
the other night when the lights were out and I
had felt something biting me. My mind was
taken off my worries when our lawyer called to
say that our baby officially belonged to us.
She wanted to set up a meeting with us for
9:30 in the evening. We were reluctant to go
out that late with such an young infant and so
much money, so we agreed to meet her first
thing in the morning instead.

We then got a phone call from Mark and
Allison from the states. They were the first
to hear the good news that our adoption was
approved. It was also good news for them
because we were bringing their baby home. The
sooner we got home, the sooner they would be
reunited with their daughter. Mark told me he
called my dad and had a nice conversation with
him. He advised us to stay near the phone
around 7 p.m. because dad would try to call

us. Dad did call and it was super to hear his voice, especially because we could tell him that he was a grandfather again. I reminded him that the battle was only half over and we still needed his prayers. I got to sleep a little easier that night even though we were still in the dark, since the landlord never came to fix the light.

Tuesday June 4th: We waited anxiously for over an hour at our lawyer's home to pay her legal fees and collect our documents. Our lawyer charged us $4,800 because we told her that was all we could afford. Knowing we had the extra money that Maria had given us, we chose to give it to our lawyer as a gesture of our honesty. To us, it symbolized that even though so many people in Romania may be corrupt, we were not. We wanted to walk away from this ordeal as honest as when we first arrived. Our American attorney had taken our money and given us only a false sense of security and nothing more. It was the Romanian lawyer who gave us exactly what she promised. We felt she deserved the money and if we had any extra cash, we would have gladly given it to her. We were upset however, to discover that all of our documents were not translated into English. Because those papers were essential to apply for the visa, we asked that it be done right away.

We hurried to the United States Embassy to have the immigration officials examine Juliana, which was among the many things that was required of us. While at the Embassy, we applied for Juliana's official health examination. Having some of her documents allowed us to progress in the adoption process. We raced to the hospital to make her 2:15 appointment, but once we got there, they informed us that no appointments would be

145

taken after noon. Once again, we went in with a nice gift for the clerk in charge of making appointments. We gave him a one pound can of coffee and a canned ham. These gifts allowed us to be seen by the doctor within minutes. We felt guilty going ahead of the sickly people we saw waiting in line.

The examination consisted of undressing Juliana and placing her on a table where the doctor examined her body. She then looked inside of her mouth and said, "Done." That one minute check-up cost us $13. We of course gave the doctor gifts for what was apparently her idea of a more professional examination. I was glad that poor Juliana didn't have to suffer through some horrible examination. It was quick and painless and that was exactly what I wanted. I only wanted the doctor to put her rubber stamp on the paper for the Embassy. Every paper completed meant we were one step closer to going home. I guarded each document with my life because if we lost just one form, or her birth certificate, who knew what that would have meant for us. In any event, we were not going to risk finding out.

The taxi ride from the hospital back to the apartment was one of the scariest rides I had ever taken in my life. The driver took us through what appeared to be worst section of Bucharest. I didn't recognize where we were and I thought for sure we were going to be robbed. I know tears were streaming down my face as I was bracing myself for the worst. I envisioned them hitting Pat on the head and stealing Juliana and all of our money. I started praying out loud as I feared we were racing nearer and nearer to our deaths. I looked over my shoulder to see if Mary was with us and she was not. I believed we were really going to die! I looked at Pat with panic written all over my face, and though he appeared calmer than me, he was scared too. I shouted to the driver, "Where are we, I don't recognize this section of town?" Just then I did recognize where we were. He must have taken us on a shortcut through the jungles of Bucharest. The only thing it seemed he shortened was our lives – by about ten years. When Pat and I got out of the car we embraced each other, and knew we were lucky to have survived another treacherous taxi ride.

After our dinner, Pat took a taxi to the lawyer's to get the translated documents necessary to apply for Juliana's visa. I stayed behind to wait for the landlord to fix the lights that were once again not working. It was a nuisance to be forced to sit in the dark night after night. Pat had been reading a novel by candle light, and I was afraid he was ruining his eyesight. It must have taken the landlord over an hour to repair and change the light bulb.

I must have sat alone in that apartment for several hours waiting for Pat, scared to death that something might have happened to him. There was a terrific thunder and lightning storm and all I could think of was Pat out there in it, with little money, no passport, no real identification, and it was getting very late. I was worried sick that something had gone wrong, when at 11 p.m., he finally returned. I was never so glad in all of my life to see him. We had lights and Juliana's papers, so we stayed up until we read every last document. It was moving for us to learn about her background and why she was placed for adoption.

Having her papers, we felt a bit more confident that we were another step closer to going home. That was a load off of our minds.

We found it difficult to sleep. I didn't know whether it was due to the mattress or because of my bug bites which were getting much worse. I was afraid that if they got infected, I would be in a real jam without proper medical help. I had three huge welts that measured about four inches in diameter. The sores were red, swollen, and feverish, and the centers were turning black. I was sure that it was these strange bites that were causing the night sweats I was having. I had to remain focused on finishing the paperwork to enable us to finalize the adoption, but the bug bites, or whatever they were, really scared me because they were getting so big and I was so far from good medical treatment.

Wednesday June 5th: Pat was the first one up and out of bed that morning. Upon entering the kitchen he discovered a dozen or so huge cockroaches had actually been the first to rise and shine. I hate bugs, especially cockroaches. These fellows were quite large too, and I wondered if they were the bugs that had bitten me. Since the night before, the bites on my legs had gotten even bigger and uglier. I felt very nauseous and notably weaker. I tried to keep my mind off of it, but it was hard not to think about it when I felt so lousy.

One thing that I didn't let my deteriorating condition do was slow me down in the paperwork chase. After breakfast, we hurried to the lawyer's office to have them assist us in obtaining Juliana's passport. It took the entire morning to get the passport. Pat and I felt as if we were tagging along in our lawyer's shadow and spending much of the time merely waiting for her to do all of the negotiating. We accepted Juliana's passport with great pride as Pat tucked it in his money belt safely next to his. Unfortunately, that was all of the work we could do on the adoption.

On our way back to the apartment we stopped in the Lido restaurant for lunch. Actually we only had an appetite for a bowl of soup and rolls. We felt terribly out of place eating in the extravagant dining room which turned into a disco dance club at night. There were at least ten different servers and waiters assigned to us, most of the lads under the age of twelve. The service was excellent, the food was superb, and the atmosphere was delightful. When we asked for our bill, we were told, "No bill, pay what you like." We knew Americans over pay for everything, yet we had no idea how much money to leave on the table. We eventually decided on 300 lei; $1.80. That was a "first" for us, as no one has ever let us decide what we wanted to pay for our meal before.

It didn't take long before the food I had just eaten started to disagree with me. To get my mind off of feeling sick, we decided to shop. Shopping always takes my mind off of my worries and problems. I bought a few dresses for 300 lei each. I found a beautiful painting of a farm girl in the window of a small shop. I wanted to buy it to hang in Juliana's room back home. I thought that she might cherish it someday. The shopkeeper was a burly type of a man and didn't appreciate me trying to speak his native tongue when I asked to buy the picture. In English he told me it was not for sale. I couldn't believe it because there were several identical pictures on display inside of the shop. When I pointed that out to him the man became infuriated. He screamed at me, "You Americans come to our country and think you can buy anything you want, well you can not. This picture is not for sale, now get out of my shop." I was enraged and could feel my blood boil as we stormed out of the store mumbling every obscenity we knew. I was a lunatic out of control. I took every ounce of my stress and frustration out on him. I gave new meaning to the phrase "Ugly American." I couldn't believe that he wouldn't sell me the lousy picture. He was a man of principle however. At home, or under different circumstances, I am sure I would have respected him for his scruples. I hated him for not selling me the picture. After all, he obviously needed the money as he was never going to unload the junk he had in that store. Yet he wouldn't sell himself out for a dollar. The image of that sweet farm girl, with the yellow scarf holding down her brown locks of hair, would remain forever in my mind.

When we returned to our apartment, I became enraged when I discovered that our light bulbs blew again. I was not going to sit in the dark one more night. I called the landlord screaming at him like a wild woman. I shouted at him, "I want lights tonight, and bring a spare lamp for an emergency." He did fix the light again and did bring a spare, but it really didn't seem to give off a whole lot of light. We only had two 60-watt bulbs dangling from a fifteen-foot-high ceiling. They were encased in an orange globe which gave an amber glow to the room. The lack of light in the apartment gave me eye strain. I am sure that it was one of the contributing factors to my constant headaches, not to mention the stress.

The best part of the whole day was when we received a phone call from Pat's mom. It was a terrible connection but her voice sounded like heaven. I felt as if I was drowning and she was throwing me a life-raft. We didn't even talk long enough for Pat to say hello, but that was all we needed. Hearing the voice of a loved one seemed to take away the stress we were under, allowing us to unwind long enough to fall asleep.

Thursday June 6th: After we took our daily ice cold showers, we stopped at a Gypsy flower stand and bought five dozen red and yellow roses to give to our lawyers to say thank you from the bottom of our hearts. The flowers only cost 300 lei and were so bountiful that they were difficult to carry. It was our way of expressing our gratitude for allowing us to have the family that we had tried to achieve for over eight long years. No words could ever say just how grateful we were for what a wonderful thing she did for not only us, but for so many other children that she placed in good homes throughout the world. Even though we were extremely glad that things were progressing in such a favorable manner, one set of documents were still not translated nor were they certified. Pat and I were devastated, for we knew that meant that we would miss our scheduled flight home. We were still glad to be so close to going home. At least the end was in sight. Nevertheless, we were very disappointed.

Every day that passed, I seemed to be feeling worse with the bug bites, and I didn't know how much longer I could go without medical treatment. I had as many as ten bites, mostly all located on my rear-end. Once again, I tried to put it out of my mind by spending the afternoon at Robin and Dave's apartment. It was interesting how all of the women gathered in the kitchen and discussed our life stories in such detail. We discovered that all of the women had suffered with cancer prior to going to Romania. We realized that it was dealing with those hardships at home that helped to make us tough enough to endure the pains of a Romanian adoption. We all agreed that we felt a common bond to each other, and promised to stay friends once we returned to our "normal" lives back home. Although our stories differed somewhat, we shared one thing for certain. We had all paid our dues, one way or another, in the struggle to get a baby out of the country.

Friday June 7th: The previous evening, Pat went to pick up our translated documents so that we could get them certified first thing in the morning. When we arrived at the court house, I was paralyzed upon seeing the building. It was the same place where Auriel's birth parents had tried to rip us off. It was at that time that I became despondent when I realized that we were going home without him. It was hard enough to concentrate on finishing up Juliana's papers without the gut-wrenching and guilt-stricken feeling that we had given up too easily on poor Auriel. Our thoughts turned to the present when we got our certifications. We felt relieved that our time at the court house was brief. Some couples had to wait days for their certifications. We gave our helper a cosmetic bag that was filled with an assortment of lipsticks and other tidbit items. It was amazing how quickly work could be accomplished with a gift.

We raced to the United States Embassy only to wait for over two hours to request an appointment for Juliana's visa. Our allotted time was four days away. I was so disappointed as our scheduled flight out of Romania was for Monday, and we couldn't get our visa appointment until Tuesday. That not only meant four extra days in that city, but hassles to change our flights. I felt very weak from my bug bites and I considered pleading with the Embassy officials for a sooner date. I was warned that if I created too many hassles for the Consulate, they could deny my visa altogether, which would mean staying in Bucharest even longer. I couldn't determine what was the lesser of two evils. Eventually I decided to gamble on waiting it out for another four days. I thought for sure I could hang on just a little bit longer. If I had suffered over a week without medical treatment, what was another four days?

As we were leaving the Embassy, we ran into our friends Steve and Carol and their two daughters who had found out that their visas had been denied. They were out of money and food, and had been struggling for over two months. I didn't know how they managed to keep going. We were able to get some food for them from a couple from Syracuse who were leaving Bucharest and had extra food to give away. Thanks to Maria, we had enough to eat. Pat and I wanted to get the food to Steve and Carol because we remembered how the food cheered us up when Maria gave us her leftover goodies before she returned to the states. We made arrangements to get together with them later on.

Our first priority was to find the Swissair office and change our flights to Thursday which was the next available flight out of Bucharest. Because we had to wait until Tuesday for the visa appointment and Thursday for our flight, we were forced to spend another week in Bucharest. I felt so close to going home, yet it seemed so far away. I only hoped I would make it.

Often when we were feeling particularly lonely, we would go to the United States Embassy just to see the American flag and be near other Americans. Support, stories and ideas were freely exchanged at the Embassy by the Americans adopting children. It amazed us how many couples we talked to who had hired the same U.S. attorneys we initially hired. Not one couple who we spoke with had success using that firm. We were outraged that a group of American lawyers would prey on desperate couples who were willing to do just about anything to adopt a child.

It was at the Embassy that we met Tony, a psychologist from California. He shared all kinds of wisdom with us including where to find a few good restaurants. Tony was adopting a baby from northern Romania and was ahead of us in the paperwork. He was therefore able to offer advice to us on ways to improve our documentation.

People like us even traded baby supplies at the Embassy. We learned of a sick child in need of Pedialyte, so we gave our only bottle to that couple hoping it would help their child. We only had three outfits and one pair of socks for Juliana so we exchanged our larger sized clothes for smaller ones.

It was rare that we heard of fortunate couples who completed their adoptions in less than two weeks. The majority of us struggled at least a month or two. We met several couples who had spent over three months working on their adoptions. We were never able to stay at the Embassy very long for it became too depressing to hear so many sad stories from couples struggling with their adoption process. One day while we were socializing with friends there, we saw a father and daughter team fighting to get their

154

exit visas. Documents were somehow misplaced at the Embassy. This father was so angry that his face was beet red. I thought he would have a heart attack and die before the government officials would help him. The frustrating issue was that most Americans anticipated, to some degree, the fighting that would be necessary to complete a foreign adoption. What we found astonishing was the fact that many of us were also fighting with the United States officials. We didn't expect to run into inadequacies and incompetencies at the Embassy. We, like many, were too naive to believe that the American Consulate could present another road of red tape for the adopting couples to be forced to battle through.

There were many functions of the Embassy as it pertained to adoptions. They were responsible for the safety of Americans who were visiting Romania. They also provided current and reliable information regarding the political unrest by issuing travelers advisories. They reported day to day accounts of the adoption status as well as processing all adoption paperwork, including issuing visas. Consulate officials were responsible for determining whether or not orphans were truly abandoned. Under immigration law, a child was not considered an orphan if the natural parents exercised any parental control of the child. While we were in Romania, that gray zone meant to many of us that we couldn't adopt a child if the father's name was on the birth certificate. We were painfully aware that when we were trying to adopt Auriel, that his birth certificate included the names of a birthmother and father. We knew that Auriel's visa would probably have been denied, even though he was clearly abandoned in an orphanage with the endorsement of the Commission. Many couples were unfairly denied their child's visa because of that gray zone. The U.S. government granted such children Humanitarian Parole stating that the adopting parents unintentionally adopted non-orphans.

Saturday June 8th: We slept in until 9 a.m. and had a delicious coffee cake that we bought at the bakery right around the corner. I only wished we had some good Paul de Lima coffee to go with it. We were down to Tang and ice tea mix. After an ice cold shower, who needs coffee to wake up? We hailed a taxi to take us to Steve and Carol's apartment. They lived farther away from the city than us, but their apartment was like a palace compared to ours for the same amount of money. It was huge, four rooms with two bathrooms, and it was bright and clean. We were glad that they had found such a nice apartment. It was just our bad luck that we rented our apartment from a bachelor who didn't keep up with house-cleaning.

They were delighted with the food we brought them. We also brought them all of our dirty clothes. Steve knew of a dry cleaner that would professionally clean our clothes for less than one dollar. We were elated as we were getting tired of washing out our clothes. With our apartment being as damp as it was, our things took several days to dry. After a brief visit we all squeezed into a taxi and went out for pizza. On our way into the pizza place Steve pointed out a bread line that was over a half a mile long. We couldn't believe our eyes. After we ate our pizza, there were poor Gypsy children who would run up to our tables and eat the food scraps that we left behind. Those children broke my heart. Steve and Carol left us to buy

156

chickens for their dinner at a nearby market, but they promised to meet with us the next day with our clean clothes.

Later that evening we went out to dinner with a group of Americans to the Continental Hotel. We heard rumors that the Continental Hotel was a popular meeting place for members of the PLO. I looked at other guests suspiciously and wondered if we were safe. Eventually my paranoia diminished with each glass of wine that I drank. We all ate fantastic meals that cost almost nothing considering how much we had to eat. For a moment, we forgot where we were and why we were in Romania. It was wonderful to enjoy ourselves while escaping the adoption fiascoes we all left behind. We all enjoyed the evening so much that we hated to see it end.

On our walk back to our apartments, we found a scale on the sidewalk and for one lei, we could see how much we weighed. The only problem was that we only had a single one lei coin. We all climbed onto the scale, acting as if we were a bunch of silly teen-agers. People were watching us as if we were drunk, and maybe we were. We all needed a night where we could forget about our adoption worries and have honest to goodness fun. For once, we went to bed with smiles on our faces. When we woke up we were still smiling, until we realized that we left our umbrella at the restaurant. Bucharest was so rainy, we knew it would be hard to survive without it. It was inevitable that we had to return and look for our umbrella. We were lunatics to believe that for one moment someone would turn in a lost umbrella when they were so hard to come by. As we had presumed, the umbrella was gone.

While we were there, we had wonderful

omelets for breakfast in the beautiful restaurant where we had eaten dinner the previous evening. When we asked for our check we were told the food was free to guests who stay in the hotel. We told the waiter we were not guests, and he became furious with us as if we just committed a crime. The man demanded $5 each for the meal. I was outraged. I shouted at him, "We have no American dollars, only 300 lei and that is all we can give." We threw the dirty bills on the table and angrily walked out.

# Chapter 10
# Say Good-bye for Me

---

On Sunday, June 9th, I knew if we were at
home we would be in church. We went to
several Orthodox churches to ask God to keep a
watchful eye over us and to help us along our
way. As I watched the other people around me,
I knew they too had favors to ask of God, and
I wondered how God could possibly listen to us
all. I somehow knew that the people I shared
the holy water with had many more problems
than I, for I knew we would be going home,
back to America soon, and this episode would
all be behind us. Yet, the Romanians that
prayed there, would continue to say the same
prayers over and over, and I wondered if their
lives would ever get better.

Every day that passed, I developed more
welts. They were getting so big and scary
looking. I was afraid to think of what I had.
Sometimes I couldn't help it because I felt so
miserable. I wondered if a poisonous spider
bit me. I wondered if I was becoming septic.
Would I make it out of Romania alive before I
lapsed into a coma? I had to get home – it
was an emergency. I tried to walk around the
city for as long as I could before I became
too weak to take another step. We returned to
our apartment where Pat made spaghetti and
beefstick for dinner. If we pretended, it was
almost like home, but after I ate it, I was
sick from it. I wondered if the bug bites
were making me sick to my stomach too. I only

wanted to go to sleep so I would forget how bad I felt. Sleeping was something that didn't come easy in the apartment, for we were afraid to close our eyes.

Monday June 10th: When I woke up I felt as if I were half dead. My body was so sore, it was difficult for me to move. I had to force myself to get up and to get dressed. We were depressed when we realized this was the day we had hoped to leave. I could only pray that somehow I would feel better on Tuesday for the visa interview. Robin called and asked us to baby sit Jason while she and Dave went to court. I wanted to die, yet I was willing to do it for her because it was the right thing to do. On our way to their apartment two men tried to pick our pockets. I was so angry I screamed at them at the top of my lungs. If I had a gun, I knew I would have shot them without thinking twice about it. Living in Romania under the circumstances that we had been faced with filled us with rage and animosity.

The day seemed to fly by for us. A friend came by to visit and she brought candy bars and a can of pop similar to Sprite called Zit. It was not a very nutritional lunch for us, but it was a rare treat. If it made us feel good, I couldn't see what was wrong with it. When Robin and Dave returned they told us how poorly they were treated by the judge who was processing all of their adoption paperwork. Apparently, they were going to have to do a song and a dance to push the papers through. In reality, we all had to do some sort of song and dance to accomplish tasks while in Romania. They also brought home an infant girl. I gave them a lot of credit for adopting two children. I wish we had planned ahead to adopt more than one child.

I was starting to feel very sick so we returned to our apartment. Something seemed out of place and different. Much to our surprise there was a refrigerator in the kitchen. It was great to have, but I wished we had had it several weeks earlier. I was paranoid that the apartment was bugged because I had frequently complained that we needed a refrigerator.

We also learned that Mark decided not to wait for us to bring his baby home for him. He would actually be in Romania that night with plans to leave first thing in the morning. I felt bad that we were not able to help him, but in a way, it was really a blessing for us as I was so sick I didn't know how I would make it home with one baby, let alone two.

Tuesday June 11th: This was the day we had been waiting for, I knew it was all up to me. I felt as if the weight of the world rested on my shoulders. I hated that pressure, but we heard from other Americans that when women request the visas, they were denied less frequently than men. I knew I had to do it by myself. We made it to the Embassy by 8:30 a.m. and as always, there was a long line outside. I waved my passport to the non-English speaking guard and said, "I have an appointment for a visa, please open the gate." And he did! I was waiting for him to push me aside and say something like, "Wait your turn," or "Get to the end of the line," but I was wrong.

Pat and I sat in total silence once inside the Embassy, patiently waiting for my name to be called. I said a million prayers and I knew my heart would break in half if our visa was denied. All the right words would be essential for this meeting. I was battling

161

with my heart so it wouldn't take control of
my mind. I wanted to be as sharp as a tack
for any of the questions I might be asked.
Quietly rehearsing my answers, everything
inside the Embassy seemed to distract me. I
thought about all the other couples who had
been in the Embassy waiting room before me,
wondering how they felt, wondering how they
made it out. All of them eventually did, some
quicker than others. I thought about Auriel
and I wondered what would ever become of him,
and that made me cry. When I looked around
the room I noticed that other people were
crying too. So many tears had been shed in
Romania over the resolving of the so called
problem of the "lost children." At least we
would be getting Juliana out. With any luck
at all, she would be going to America. If I
could only get her a visa.

I saw new folks just arriving in the
country, making their way into the U.S.
Embassy trying to start the adoption process.
I recalled how I felt when I first arrived. I
looked at all the haggard people trying to get
visas to get home, and there I was at last.
It had seemed if that day would never arrive
and then I heard it. My name echoed
throughout the walls and slowly I worked my
way through the hordes of people, trying to
find booth number three. I looked back at Pat
before I entered the booth, and the look on
his face told me a million things about how
much he loved me, and how much faith he had in
me to get the visa. I felt as if I was on
trial and my life depended on the outcome of
the hearing. The questions were many, but
relatively painless. Before I knew it I heard
the words, "Visa approved." Tears immediately
welled in my eyes and I thanked them over and
over explaining that I was just so grateful to

162

be going home. I would have kissed their feet if they had let me.

I showed very little emotion as I left booth number three as I knew there were couples all around me that were being denied. I wanted to respect their feelings. I held Pat close to me as I whispered in his ear that we were going home. It was so emotional knowing that we had finally done it and it was over. We quickly walked down the street and when we got to the corner, we allowed ourselves time to express the joy that we were suppressing. There was another woman standing there and she too had had her visa approved. Though we didn't even know her, we all stood there and hugged each other as we cried on each other briefly. It was hard to believe that we were finally going home.

We had the remainder of the day to enjoy until we were required to return to the Embassy at closing time to pick up the actual visa. We thought it would be a wonderful idea for us to visit the museum where the Romanian crown jewels were on display. It was very impressive, and for a brief moment, I thought I was in London looking at the crown jewels of England. We also walked to The People's Palace which was Ceausescu's monumental mansion to himself and his ideology. It was scary to be near it. It's mammoth size alone intimidated us. I can not explain the feeling one gets standing so near it. It would be similar to the feeling one might have when standing next to Hitler's house.

We also did a little more shopping. At that point, Pat and I were able to communicate quite well with the Romanian people. We were trying to learn how to speak the language. It was definitely making shopping easier and a lot more fun. I also felt a little more brave about going places, as I knew where to go and where not to go. I knew I would miss the shopping. I knew I would also miss the ladies in the bakery around the corner from our apartment – perhaps even more than their puff pastries. I was getting to know them quite well, and they recognized us every time we entered their shop.

I was not feeling well, so I took a nap while Pat took a taxi to Steve and Carol's apartment. They were late returning our clean clothes and we were getting worried since we were out of things to wear. Much to our surprise, the laundromat claimed our clothes were stolen, so Pat returned without them. We found a store where clothes were shipped in from Canada and we bought an outfit to wear home. It was not expensive and the store manager kissed our hands as we left.

We placed a call to Lili. We had not seen her in quite some time. We asked her to take us to the mountains the following day as it was going to be our last day in Romania. I didn't want to go touring because I was so sick and didn't feel up to a trip. I pictured the car breaking down causing us to miss our flight. Pat really wanted to travel, so I would go for his sake.

We returned to the Embassy to get Juliana's visa at the end of the day. It felt fantastic once I had it in my hands. All of our tears and month's worth of trials and tribulations had been sealed in a big brown envelope. I knew all of the adoption papers and everything we had collected for them were in there. We certainly did an awful lot of work to get that package. There was no doubt in my mind that after our adoption experience, childbirth would be too easy for me.

I thought about all the emotional and

164

physical pain that we had to endure. For
eight long years we had worked toward having a
family and in this far away land, it was all
coming together for us. The entire ordeal
made me very bitter because of all of the pain
and hardships we had had to deal with. I
couldn't stop thinking about how my sister
would have her "miracle" baby in a nice clean,
safe hospital, where nurses would take care of
her and the baby.

Our experience allowed me the opportunity
to reflect on the depth of the love I feel for
Pat and what a wonderful husband, friend, and
partner he is. I recall one evening when I
was feeling so sick, Pat insisted that I drink
the last of the water we had brought from
home. He always gave me the best of
everything in Romania, and if anyone deserved
the husband of the year award, it would be
him. While many husbands had to return to the
states to their jobs or other responsibilities, Pat stayed with me until the bitter
end. Pat's shoulders carried not only the new
responsibilities of fatherhood and all of his
worries, but all of mine too. I couldn't have
done it without him.

Dad called to see how we were coming along
in the paperwork. It felt colossal when I
exclaimed, "We're coming home." I couldn't
wait to say those words. I knew eventually I
would get to say them, but I had no idea how
happy it would really make us feel to say
them. I said them over and over and over.
When I laid down to go to sleep that night, I
was the happiest over getting out of the
apartment. I couldn't wait to sleep in a real
bed, with clean sheets. I fell asleep
repeating, "Only two more nights in this
filthy apartment, only two more nights."

Wednesday June 12th: Pat took a taxi to

165

the Swiss Embassy to get Juliana a transit visa as I waited at the InterContinental Hotel for Steve and Carol to see if they ever found our clothes. Steve knew that the manager of the dry cleaners had stolen our clothes, so he bullied his way into the establishment and looked through all of the clothes. When he found Woolrich shirts and Calvin Klein underwear, he knew he had our stuff. What a wonderful surprise it was to be able to wear a clean outfit on our trip into the mountains. That was to be the last time we would see Steve and Carol. Our prayers and thoughts for them would remain with us for a long time.

I tried to walk back to the apartment carrying both the baby and the laundry. I realized that I didn't have any strength left, so I sat on the street corner in the rain and waited for Lili. She helped me back to the apartment where I then showed her the bites. I had over fifteen welts. Lili thought they were spider bites. I told her I saw a rat the size of a small dog in the courtyard of our apartment and was worried that rats were in our apartment and bit us as we slept on the floor. She didn't know what to tell me, and she could clearly see how sick I was. She got us situated and in no time Pat returned with the Swiss transit visa and we were on our way to the Sub-Carpathian Mountains.

It really was a good idea to get out of the city and get some fresh air. The car we had was a sturdier vehicle than the others we had been in, and I felt more comfortable knowing that this Dacia probably wouldn't break down. I was not sure if the ride was in fact any better, or if I was merely getting used to Romanian cars and Romanian drivers. We were getting familiar with the roads and the scenery.

The north country was much more picturesque than the trip we had taken to the eastern part of Romania when we first arrived. As we traveled further and further north, the countryside was becoming more and more beautiful. The rolling hills were changing into majestic mountains that were landscaped with vibrant-colored wildflowers and white snow-capped peaks. The two-story houses we saw along the way were painted in a Bavarian style. Lili was taking us to a resort town named Sinaia, but I felt like I was in Switzerland. Keeping in mind that we had been cooped up in a dump in Bucharest for several weeks, and taking into consideration that I was feverishly ill, to me it was as good as Switzerland.

We visited Peles Castle, which had been built by the royal Romanian family back in the late 1800's when the country was a monarchy under the rule of King Ferdinand and Queen Marie. We would rank that castle right along with the many other more famous ones that we have had the opportunity to visit in Great Britain. It felt absolutely wonderful to breath in the fresh mountain air. I forgot how good it was to breath fresh air. All along the way the scenery was simply spectacular, and the towns were adorable. Every mountain town had a picture-postcard look to it. I couldn't believe that I was still in Romania.

Lili knew of a restaurant that was located at the top of one of the mountains. It took over a half an hour to reach it as we traveled up the winding, washed out, rocky road. The view was spectacular, but the meal was awful. We didn't care because it was rejuvenating being away from the big city. The cool mountain air had a refreshing chill to it, and

I couldn't help but to think that it was the first time in a long time that I allowed my body's blood to be oxygenated with something other than pollutants.

We had our first taste of Tzuica, Romania's famous plum brandy. I didn't enjoy it but Lili and the driver had definitely acquired a taste for it. Pat however, sampled Romania's premium Azuga beer which was made in that region. Even though I still didn't feel well, being there made me feel better, even a little bit healthier. It was getting late and I was getting extremely anxious to return to Bucharest. Maybe it was the thin mountain air that caused me to sense a roaring headache coming on. I knew I had either given my brain too much clean air for one day, or I was getting sicker. It was agony for me to endure the long ride back to Bucharest. The car had a much easier time going home since it was all downhill. It took less than three hours, but it seemed like eternity. Knowing that it would be our last journey out in the countryside, we captured the images along the way in our minds as well as taking an occasional photograph.

Once in Bucharest, we gave Lili a big hug and a kiss good-bye. We gave her one of our suitcases filled with all of our left over clothes and gifts knowing that she could use those things more than us. We promised to keep in touch, but I doubted that we ever would. I wasn't sure why. Maybe it had something to do with the fact that she was so reluctant to help us in the beginning when we needed her most. We both realized that Lili's wish to become a tour guide indeed came true, for during our adoption search and struggle in Romania, that was all that she was to us, a tour guide.

We spent the rest of the evening with the group of Americans that we had become such good friends with. It was really going to be hard for us to leave them behind. I only hoped and prayed that soon they would follow us. All of us went out to dinner to one of our favorite spots, the Continental Hotel. It wasn't the same though. We were sad to be leaving our friends behind. Our tables were lacking the spirit and animation that was visible throughout the rest of the restaurant. We knew that everyone had the weight of the world, or at least Romania, on their shoulders. There were no words to describe how happy I was to be going home, but my heart went out to our friends knowing that they had to endure the rest of their stay there with fewer and fewer Americans. Pat and I walked back to our apartment after we said our good-byes, holding hands while we walked in silence. We both knew that it was these people who had made our stay there more tolerable. Leaving wouldn't have been possible without them. Our stay wouldn't have been possible without them either.

When we returned to our lifeless, shadowless apartment we saw a four inch long cockroach scurry when we turned on the kitchen light. I knew that I couldn't take another night there. I could make it only if I kept telling myself that we would be going home in one day. I couldn't believe that only a moment ago we were so distraught over leaving our friends behind. I couldn't think of anything other than getting the hell out of that God-forsaken place. I would only have to sleep on the floor surrounded by filth for one more night. I couldn't believe it. I became overwhelmed by terrible thoughts such as, what if our flight was canceled and we would have to spend another night there? I really thought I would die.

We had given all of our left-over food, toilet paper, and soaps to Dave and Robin. Since we had given away all of our clothes as well, we had very little packing to do. It took us less than five minutes to pack two bags for Juliana; one with souvenirs for her, and the other with baby supplies. We took a moment to lie in bed and reflect on our tour of Romania. It definitely was the most different, yet enlightening, experiences of our lives. I prayed that in time the bitterness, pain, and sadness would go away. I know it may take years, perhaps a lifetime to get over our Romanian journey. I hoped we could feel somewhat normal once we returned home. It was impossible for me to think I would be "like I was before" after living in Romania. I knew that I had to accept that our Romanian experience had changed our lives forever, and there was no getting over that. I hoped our families would understand it, though we really didn't expect them to.

In a way, it was like someone who spent time in Vietnam coming home and trying to tell us what it was like. We could sympathize, but we would never really know the pain that they felt while on their tour and how the war had affected them. Only others who had shared the same experiences would be able to empathize. The people that had touched our lives while in Romania would remain a part of our lives and family. While others wouldn't be able to fully comprehend what we lived through, Robin and Dave, Mark and Allison, Steve and Carol, Irene, and all of the others would understand. We all had a common bond between us - one that would keep us together for years to come.

Thursday June 13th: We thought we would

170

sleep in on our last morning. Our peaceful dawn was cut short by the sound of the telephone ringing next to our heads as we lay in bed. The wake up call was from our friendly local landlord. At first I thought, in my half-awake state, that he was calling to wish us well and to have a safe trip home. When I heard him ask in his mediocre English for another ten dollars in rent, I quickly arose from bed. He felt that we should pay for spending the greater part of the day in his place. I was really furious, but there it was, our last day, and I didn't need another fight. I didn't have the strength to fight him, but he was morally wrong to demand payment for a room we were only planning to be in until noon. (Isn't that usually the normal check out time?) It was our last Romanian ripoff before our departure. I should have planned on something like that happening, but I still had too much faith in mankind.

We had hired Mario in advance to drive us to the airport. He was the very first person we had met when we first arrived into Romania. We thought he might as well be the last person we talked to as well. It was a very emotional ride to the airport, because I couldn't stop remembering how I had felt on my initial ride in. We passed the same rows of flowers and apartment dwellings, the same signs and logos. A military air show above hinted that we were nearing the airport. We knew Mario's car was due for another repair shop appointment because it shimmied down the highway. Our journey was about to come to an end. We had suffered the ultimate journey to hell, and going home was all we cared about. We had experienced so much and I wondered if the emotional scars would haunt me for the rest of my life. Every time I would look at Juliana,

171

I couldn't believe that we had pulled this thing off, and we had the most beautiful baby in the world in our arms. Juliana was healthy and I estimated that she had gained several pounds. She had been a very good baby, crying only to let us know that she was hungry. Between the three of us, Juliana actually cried the least.

We gave Mario the rest of our lei since it was illegal to leave the country with it. We kept only one clean, crisp bill as a souvenir. Pat gave him a suit jacket that he had brought over and he hugged him good-bye. As the time approached for us to leave, I held Juliana a little tighter as we climbed the stairs to the big silver bird that would carry us back to America. Before I walked down the narrow isle to find my seat, I turned back for one last look. I waved an emotional farewell as the sun burned into the horizon. When I looked down at Juliana her big brown eyes seemed to ask me to say good-by for her. As we were filled with peace, Juliana drifted off to sleep and our plane headed westward through the billowy clouds that seemed to cradle us. We felt like we were in God's territory and he would take care of us and get us home safely.

The extra money we paid for the Swissair flight was worth every penny. We were treated like royalty. I was becoming even more ill as we flew off, and I couldn't understand why my health was rapidly deteriorating. I knew I would be home in a few days. All of the fighting was over, and I could finally relax, so why was I getting sicker? Subconsciously, I let my guard down on the flight, and that made me realize how sick I was. While in Romania, I could never let my guard down, not even for one minute. I somehow wondered if I was that sick all along, and I was starting to

172

understand the magnitude of the illness. When I thought about that, I could almost make myself believe that I was overreacting.

I tried to concentrate on the wonderful aspects of the flight. For one thing, I was given an entire six-pack of diet Coke, with ice, and a whole box of Swiss chocolates. That was like heaven. Airline food never really tasted that great, but the food on that particular flight was exceptionally good. We ate everything on our plates for once. That food was obviously better than the freeze-dried camper meals that we had eaten for several weeks and had grown accustomed to. Swissair catered to the adopting couples. We needed it and appreciated it after all we had been through in Romania.

By the time we made it to our hotel in Zurich, Switzerland, I was almost in septic shock. I knew that I had something really bad, and it was only a matter of time before it brought me totally down. I was hallucinating from the moment we got into the elevator that took us to our room. I was in disbelief that the elevator had lights. I cried out to total strangers, "I can't believe that we don't have to ride in pitch darkness." When we got out of the elevator, I screamed once again, "The halls are lit, and it's clean, and there's carpet on the floor. I can't believe how well lit this place is." I could barely walk, even though poor Pat was holding me up. He was also carrying all of the luggage as well as the baby. He was really struggling and could tell that I was losing it.

I couldn't keep my mouth shut. I went on to scream once we got inside our room and saw what a palace it was. It was so bright and clean. It even had MTV! There was a double bed, with real crisp, clean sheets. The

173

bathroom was spacious and clean, and the shower had hot water. Pat told me I could drink the water but I wouldn't believe him. That was when I knew I was in trouble when I wouldn't even believe Pat. I tore my clothes off and laid on the bed, moaning uncontrollably. I was in so much pain I couldn't stop crying. I had twenty bites all over my stomach, legs, and rear end. Some of them were the size of grapefruits.

Pat knew that my health was rapidly deteriorating and that it was critical that I see a doctor immediately. He left me alone with the baby and ran down to the lobby to get help. He found out that before I could go to a Swiss hospital I needed a doctors referral. The reception desk contacted a local doctor who did house calls. He came to my rescue, but I didn't trust him completely. He wanted to give me injections but I wouldn't believe that the needles were clean. I couldn't understand him due to his poor English. I kept on repeating, "Allergy to penicillin, allergy to penicillin." He must have finally understood because he left and returned later with pills. He stressed to me how very important it was to take them, although he didn't know what was causing my condition.

After he left, I still wouldn't take the pills for fear that it was some type of penicillin. That was one thing I didn't need, a reaction. Pat called his brother, a pharmacist in Pennsylvania, who convinced us that the pills were safe to take. We rationalized that if I didn't take the pills I could die. If I did take the pills, they could kill me, but chances were, they wouldn't. Either way, I could die, but the pills gave me an opportunity to live. I had been through so much to have Juliana with us,

I had to take the pills for her sake.

I knew I needed rest, but I was afraid to go to sleep as I feared I would never again wake up. Pat put me to bed and promised to keep a watchful eye on me all night. I woke up one time during the night, wringing wet as if my fever had finally broken. I wanted to get out of bed to see if I could walk. With some pain and much difficulty, I could. It was then that I realized I was going to be all right. It was a little scary for a while, but I believe that it was the medication that the doctor gave me that prevented me from going into shock. I truly believed that for a moment I was going to die. So often, I would say, "I am going to get a baby, or die trying," but I never really meant it, and it nearly happened.

In the morning, I still didn't feel wonderful, but I knew I could make the flight home for American medical expertise. There was something a little unnerving about being sick and in a hospital in some foreign country. If I could make it to Boston, I would be grateful. Pat and I decided to give it a try. We ate breakfast in the hotel which was the most wonderful buffet I had ever seen.

The Swissair flight seemed to take forever. For me, it was the longest ride of my life. Juliana was incredibly wonderful, crying for only twenty minutes during the entire flight. The flight attendants were exceptionally nice to us and gave us priority over all other passengers. I stood up and danced exuberantly even though I was still very ill as we landed in Boston and passed through the gate that welcomed us to America. People must have thought I was so strange. I was so glad to be home. Tears were streaming down my face as we were escorted to the front

175

of the immigration line. All we had to say was "Romanian adoption" and we took priority over all other passengers. We were treated very well in Boston. I really appreciated it after the rough treatment in Romania. We were prepared to fight everyone at Immigration, but there was no need to. We were still in a fighting mode, and figured it would take us a while to stop wanting to fight for every little thing.

By now it was a common sight to see Romanian children at Logan airport in Boston, a main port of entry along with New York and Toronto. Juliana smiled as she posed for her first official picture taken in the USA by the Immigration officer. What a glorious welcome home!

# Chapter 11
# HOME at LAST

---

We were surrounded mostly by business people on our final one hour flight into Syracuse. I knew that our haggard appearance stood out from their wrinkled white shirts and suits. Between the two of us we had lost over 40 pounds. The soiled and baggy clothes that covered our worn down bodies must have suggested to them that we were not your ordinary vacation travelers. Pat even passed by a co-worker who didn't recognize him. (Did we really look that bad?) Pat and I carried Juliana off the plane in her wicker basket to symbolize that we had our baby together. We were greeted in the terminal by family, neighbors, and friends. It was the best homecoming anyone in the world could ever imagine.

Pat and I split up for the first time since we had started our journey. He took the baby home, and I went directly to the hospital where I was immediately rushed into surgery. The doctors chose to cut open and drain only the largest of the wounds. After 24 hours of intravenous therapy and drugs which included heavy-duty pain killers and antibiotics, I was released to my parents' care. It really felt wonderful to once again have the tender loving care of Mom and Dad. Pat's parents were already home taking care of Pat and Juliana. That was what we both needed, our parents and all of their love.

Dad drove me around the neighborhood before pulling in the drive way of our home. There was a "Welcome Home" sign on the garage door, that made me cry to see it. From now on I vowed to cry only happy tears. I was still very weak and needed help walking, so with Mom on one arm, and Dad on the other, they walked me around the house. I had really missed my house, my yard, the warm sunshine and the clean air. I wanted to be outside in it for a while before rushing in. Crying the whole time, I knew it was upsetting to my parents, as they had no idea what I had been through. They hurried me inside where the first thing I saw was my beloved dog, Sparkey. There are no words to describe how I had missed her. I could tell from the way she was acting that she had missed me too. My body was still very numb and feeble, which caused our greeting to be cut short so I could lay down to rest. My house was a mess and people were everywhere. The baby was bounced from person to person but I didn't care about one thing.

I continued to be sick for another six months with the same sores sporadically appearing out of nowhere. Along with flu like symptoms, Pat had also begun to experience similar symptoms and had a few "bites" of his own. During this time we were repeatedly seen by various physicians who had a very difficult time diagnosing our condition. We were diagnosed with a variety of aliments. I tested positive for salmonella, lyme disease, staphylococcus, and typhus. I also lost my job at the American Red Cross due to my extended illness. Because I was out of a job and trying to recover from the variety of diseases I had, I decided to write about my Romanian experience. It was such an unbelievable story. If I hadn't lived it, I wouldn't believe it myself. All I really have to do is look at Juliana's tender and gentle face, and I know that the trip was well worth it. I feel I am the luckiest person on earth to have survived Romania and to have a daughter as sweet as Juliana. For so many years I have longed for a child like this and now I finally have her. In a strange and mysterious way it makes sense to me now why we could never have children before. God wanted us to wait for Juliana. She didn't have to come from my body for me to love her. She came from my heart instead, which makes our love for her even greater.

It was during the summer of 1991 when I noticed my rosary beads had turned gold. I used to carry them with me every day to church when I was asking God to help us make our initial decision whether or not to go to Romania. I never really expected them to. It sure is special for me to hold them close to my heart after all we have been through. God has given me so many miracles. Juliana is undoubtedly one and the rosary is another. God also gave me my life back. For a while, I was not really sure of whether or not I was going to make it. Seeing the Blessed Mother for two days in Romania was also a miracle for us. It is very emotional to recall the events of the day when I saw the Blessed Mother. The day was May 21st, and the place was Buzau, a small peasant village. Coincidentally, Juliana was born on that day in Buzau. Who can explain the powers of God? Without God I know we wouldn't have Juliana with us today, and for that I feel truly blessed.

Our experiences in Romania taught us a great deal about appreciating the little things in life, those that we often take for granted. Not only physical needs such as

179

food, water, a house with lights and other
material goods, but more importantly those
things that can't be touched - only felt -
such as our freedom and simply being alive.
We are grateful to be Americans, all three of
us. After living in Romania, where every
aspect of life is controlled, we learned how
lucky we are to live in the land of the free.
Romania changed us in ways that we never
dreamed possible, but we are in fact, better
people for having lived through it. I'm glad
to say that I am no longer bitter, just
better.

We still keep in touch with all of the
couples we made friends with in Romania. The
best part about our friendship is watching
these beautiful children grow before our eyes.
It was especially wonderful during the
holidays, sending cards and pictures all over
the United States to couples we had brief
encounters with while in Bucharest. In the
Syracuse area there was a special Christmas
party for over fifty children who had been
adopted from Romania. Before we go to these
special events, I whisper into Juliana's ear
that she is getting together with her "other"
family. Like all of the parents, it really is
wonderful that the children will have each
other for support as they get older. There is
a lot of baggage that is unfairly attached to
the "lost children of Romania."

I still think of poor Auriel and I wonder
how he is. Not a day passes where he is
absent from my thoughts and prayers. Tears
quickly fill my eyes when I realize we left
Juliana's would-be brother behind. I wish we
could have found a way to bring him home with
us, and I regret having thrown in the towel so
hastily when we were in Romania. I have left
him in God's hands, and pray that he is all

180

right. A part of me wants to return to Romania to try once again to get him out of that orphanage, but for now it is financially impossible. Though our trip to Romania has left us broke, we look at Juliana and feel very rich. I don't have to have money to be rich. For me it goes way beyond money. Our lives have been enriched by all of these experiences in building our family. Our hearts are the richest of all for they are now filled with so much love. Money could never buy our happiness, but love could, and did.

I love being home with my family and friends around me. I never used to be a "home-body," but now I am. I plan to travel less and enjoy the comfort and security of my home more. I could care less when my house gets messy, after the conditions we had lived in. Our house is like a palace, and I love it more now than ever before. There really is no place like home.

Now we are living normal lives and occasionally when we hear a plane fly over head, we stop and remember our Romanian journey. Sometimes it brings tears to our eyes, but those emotions change quickly to joy as we watch Sparkey try to run after it. While most dogs chase cars, she chases airplanes. It is often said that dogs take on the characteristics of their owners and I guess that really is true. Pat and I also chase after things that most people wouldn't. The only thing is that we were lucky enough to find what we were looking for, and her name is Juliana.

# Epilogue

As time went on and Juliana transformed into an adorable toddler, our desire to have a sibling for her grew strong. We knew the doors to the adoptions were basically closed with the exception of a few children trickling into the United States through the six agencies that had been approved by the Romanian Adoption Committee. We felt the adoption scene in Romania was dismal, so we checked into Russian, Ukrainian, and Moldavian adoptions. When each of these avenues appeared to go nowhere, we somehow were always lead back to Romania.

We became active members in a national organization which provides relief to orphans in Romania. For two years we collected cases of formula, medical supplies, clothes, and toys for the children in the Buzau orphanage. We also did something that we thought we would never do - keep in touch with Lili. As time went on, we realized Lili was not to blame for the problems we faced in 1991. We looked forward to her frequent letters and hoped to see her again someday.

In the spring of 1993 I called our Romanian lawyer in Bucharest to verify if a private adoption could be done. Elena, our lawyer, assured us that it was perfectly legal but extremely difficult. She agreed to help us locate an adoptable child and reminded us that the process would take several months and cost a lot more money. We agreed to be patient and pay her inflated fees.

For the next several months we worked on our immigration paper work, we updated our homestudy, child abuse clearance, and became precertified in the New York State courts. We called Elena several times a week to check on her progress. The feedback was often discouraging and we felt as if everyone was dragging their feet while working on our adoption.

In April Elena found an adoptable baby for us. It was coincidental that our child would come from the same Buzau orphanage that we supplied aid to. The thought that we were taking care of our child without ever knowing it was too much to comprehend.

In May we received photographs of Andrea, the child we were trying to adopt. The photographs portrayed her as a sickly and lifeless being. Needless to say we wished we never saw the pictures of her. As I held the black and white photo of a helpless baby in my hands, she was slowly inching her way in my heart. I often imagined her laying day and night, month after month, with no one to hold her and no one to love her. I thought about how cold and dark the orphanage was. I thought about how her stomach must growl for food and how her heart must thirst for attention. She had no toys, no blankets, no diapers, no medicine. She had a bed and a roof over her head and not much more. She was fed two bottles of cold camomile tea each day. This child was wasting away while I sat at home and clenched my head in my hands, not ever knowing for sure if I could ever bring her home.

To make matters worse the State Department advised us not to pursue our adoption. They told us to use one of the six licensed agencies. After checking into those agencies we discovered that very few children were actually immigrating to the United States. Elena urged us not to give up on little Andrea. She told us that Andrea was a lovely child with a happy disposition. We just couldn't turn our backs on her. Yet in July I wanted to throw in the towel and allow Juliana to be raised as an only child. I repeatedly packed and unpacked our bags as our decision to go to Romania would sway from day to day.

Other deterring factors in our decision making process resulted in the fact that we didn't know any other Americans who were pursuing private adoptions in Romania. In 1991 we knew so many people who were flocking to Romania to adopt, but this time we were literally all alone. There were no families to turn to for help or support. We were also afraid that the U.S. Embassy would deny Andrea's visa. The Consulate had made it very clear to us that no private adoptions were allowed in Romania under the new law. Yet our lawyer contradicted them stating our adoption was perfectly legal. Elena told us she had a signed adoption decree in her hands. We didn't know who to believe. We were perplexed and wanted to trust the U.S. government, yet we also wanted to believe our Romanian lawyer - a woman we thought we knew and trusted.

On August 15, 1993, we followed our hearts half-way around the world in search of a little orphan girl who we called Andrea Christina. We were harboring the same fears that we felt two years before. On this trip however, we were leaving our darling Juliana with hopes that we could bring back a sister for her. We had no idea what we would find

184

once we arrived, but we knew we had to learn for ourselves if it was possible to legally adopt Andrea.

Upon arrival into the Bucharest airport we couldn't believe we were back again. We noticed that some things had changed over the past two years such as the spruced up airport. As we drove away from the center of town we noticed that time had almost stood still for the rest of Romania.

Over the past two years something else that changed was our relationship with Lili. On this trip we were eager to see her and reluctant to say good-by. Lili arranged for us to stay with her during our visit.

While we were in Romania we were prepared for heartache and disappointment - we were prepared for the worst. What we didn't expect was to complete the adoption process in less than ten days. Although we were only in Romania for such a short period of time, it still didn't compensate for the eight months of emotional turmoil and gut wrenching decisions we were forced to make.

The very first time that I looked into those big brown Romanian eyes was on August 21, 1993. It was in Elena's law office in Bucharest where we met Andrea Christina. The effects of her life in the orphanage were painfully present and it almost caused our hearts to break in half. As I slowly crept toward Andrea, dying to hold her, I knew that we both faced a long road ahead of us. Andrea never stopped rocking as I gently picked her up. It was then that I discovered in horror that our eleven month old daughter only weighed twelve pounds.

Our lawyer Elena and her sister Nicoleta were our heroes. They made it possible for us to have a family. Only two years ago we adopted Juliana through them. We met Juliana for the first time in the very same room that we met Andrea. As I stood in their office holding Andrea, the memories of 1991 raced back to me in an avalanche of pain and joy. The adoption process was completely different back then. We were thankful to God that we were blessed twice with Romanian children.

As we were leaving Romania we looked down at the beautiful countryside. We knew we were living the final chapter in our adoption saga. The next time that we fly over the barren fields would be many years from now. Perhaps we would return when our daughters grow older and want to visit their homeland.

On October 7, 1993, Andrea Christina celebrated her first birthday. Officials from the United States Department of Immigration and Naturalization Services informed us that Andrea was only the fifth child to immigrate to America through a private Romanian adoption in 1993. Despite the fact that we were uncertain about whether or not the doors to the adoptions were open, we kept our hearts open and persevered.

We feel the doors to the Romanian adoptions are beginning to open slowly to Americans once again. One thing is for certain; the adoptions in Romania will probably never be the way they were in 1991. The adoption process is a lot longer and more costly. The one who pays the dearest price however, is the child who must remain an orphan.

We have not forgotten the thousands of other children that remain in hellish conditions in so many of Romania's orphanages. We continue to provide aid to the children and are devoted to helping people adopt them.

Despite the fact that the adoption process

is often long, difficult and exhausting, it can be done and Andrea is proof of that. She may have been among the first to immigrate to America since the closing of the doors, but I know in my heart that she will not be the last.